PRIMARY HISTORY

USING THE EVIDENCE OF
THE HISTORIC ENVIRONMENT

ENGLISH HERITAGE

ABOUT THIS BOOK

To those of us working in heritage education, the most exciting new developments have been in primary history. Many teachers in primary schools have taken up the challenges of National Curriculum history and turned them into opportunities to excite pupils with a discovery of the past. But it has not just been a discovery of past cultures through textbooks. Teachers have used the past around them - in their own schools, in the locality and through the parents and grandparents of their pupils. Many schools have built up collections of locally related objects and documents. Some schools have made recordings of residents and set up projects in which their own pupils have been carrying out **real** historical detective work.

This is book has been written especially for primary teachers. As you turn its pages you will find illustrations of real evidence, help and advice to bring history alive for your pupils. Inside you will find

■ sections on historical enquiry and periods of the past specified in the National Curriculum

■ activity sheets which you can photocopy to use with your pupils in the classroom or out in the historic environment

■ case studies of places or subject areas.

Mike Corbishley,
Head of Education, English Heritage.

HISTORICAL ENQUIRY

This section introduces those areas of enquiry which your pupils will need to be familiar with. They can then make the best use of a whole range of evidence - from the high street to an ancient site.

Asking questions and finding out   4-9

The past around us looks at the layers of our past with suggestions for introducing some simple observation work.

Asking the right questions has photocopiable activities to investigate houses.

Issues raises a number of questions about the long-term conservation of our past. Should we preserve buildings just because they are old?

Visiting sites   10-15

My class is in ruins provides advice for visiting ancient sites with a photocopiable checklist to fill out before you leave school.

Take note is about simple note taking and sketching by pupils on a site - probably the simplest and easiest key skill you can teach them.

Recording gravestones encourages pupils to make accurate records of an important source of evidence, especially for a local study.

Using objects   16-19

An object lesson is all about using objects in the classroom to develop observational and analytical skills.

Object games continues the work on objects with five tried and tested games for the classroom.

Documentary evidence 20-23

Evidence from documents provides a checklist of some of the more accessible documents for you to use in the classroom or at the record office.

An eye for detail looks at one type of document - the photograph.

Interpretations of history   24-29

Interpreting history is an important part of history teaching and learning. This section provides an introduction to some of the bias in historical evidence.

An Anglo-Saxon hermitage is a **Case Study** in interpreting history.

Fabulous Fronts is an **Activity Sheet** to take the idea of interpretation into your local area.

AREAS OF STUDY: KEY STAGE 1

This section looks in detail at areas of the history curriculum which can be studied at KS1.

Looking at houses helps pupils think carefully about their own houses and, using the **Activity Sheets**, provides interesting extension work into *Now*, *Long Ago* and *Very Long Ago*.

Famous people and events suggests ways of using stories and timelines. These ideas are developed in **Big history book** and **Make a drama**.

AREAS OF STUDY: KEY STAGE 2

This section provides an introduction to each area of study at KS2. After each period introduction there is at least one Case Study.

The Romans in Britain outlines the main areas of Roman life and is followed by a **Case Study** on **A Roman Villa**, Lullingstone in Kent.

The Anglo-Saxons relates the history of their settlement in Britain, with a **Case Study** on **An Anglo-Saxon Village**, West Stow in Suffolk.

The Vikings were not just pirate warriors - they also settled large parts of Britain. The **Case Study** is of **A Viking Town**, York and the Jorvik Viking Centre.

Tudor Life outlines the Tudor period in Britain and gives the background to some of the evidence from houses and forts. The **Case Study** is of **The Tudor House** and takes as its example Kirby Hall, Northamptonshire.

Victoria's England concentrates on the life and influences of the queen and Prince Albert. There are two **Case Studies** for this period - **Victorian Civic Pride** looks at Birmingham in the Victorian period and **Life in a Country House** is a study of Brodsworth Hall, near Doncaster.

Britain since 1930 looks at the types of evidence which you can use for this period and details the major changes in people's lives, including the role of women and the changes in leisure activities.

Three **Case Studies** complete this section for KS2: **Investigating a locality** shows you how easy it is to investigate a place using documents and observation, **The impact of war** looks at the evidence of the Second World War on Dover and **The remnants of war** investigates some of the clues still to be found in our landscape for this period.

This section has a list of books and other classroom resources which you may use to take individual topics further.

THE PAST AROUND US

WHAT IS THE EVIDENCE FOR THE PAST?

'The past is all around us' is a phrase you will often have heard. But what does it mean? Put simply, it means that in Britain our environment has been shaped, altered, added to and partly destroyed many times over the centuries. In fact, since we now know that human beings were here at least half a million years ago, there has been great scope for change. We know that there are hardly any 'natural' landscapes left in Britain. You will find evidence of human occupation and use of our landscape, practically everywhere. This evidence might be very obvious for example:

■ an ancient building such as a cathedral

■ or a constructed landscape such as parkland around a country house

Padbury, Bucks, medieval ridge and furrow fields.

Audley End House, Essex.

or it might be harder to spot without help such as:

■ the remains of a medieval town plan hidden within modern town developments

■ or evidence of some ancient settlement from scatters of material, such as flints or pottery or bones, in a field, or earthworks.

IN YOUR STREET

The past is not somewhere which is a long coach journey from your school. Here is a city street which has seen many changes since the last century. Investigating the past in your own neighbourhood may allow you to make more out-of-school visits and collect resources, such as maps and other documents more easily. Pupils could draw, rather than photograph, rows of buildings like these.

LOOK OUT FOR

Building materials   Open spaces

The layers of our past

Wherever you live or teach, you will simply be inhabiting the topmost layer of the past. Where your school is, what materials it is built of, even what it is called will probably have been influenced by what or who was there before. It is sometimes hard for pupils to see the layers of the past. Too often we are told to get back into the past without any help. Have you ever heard anyone say, on an ancient site, 'Imagine what is was like as a Roman soldier/Saxon farmer /medieval monk/slave/mill worker here'? It is not easy to make that imaginative leap into the past. But there are ways of constructing 'stepping stones' which can help pupils.

Parish churches usually have had a number of additions, such as porches or chapels.

This is an obvious example of an addition to a modern house.

A clear example of a blocked-in window and a street name to investigate.

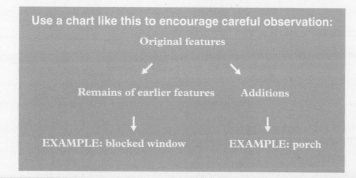

Use a chart like this to encourage careful observation:

Original features

Remains of earlier features   **Additions**

EXAMPLE: blocked window   **EXAMPLE: porch**

■ Travel back into the past from the present. Start where your pupils are - in their homes or in the school classroom.

■ Encourage your pupils to think about the shape of a familiar environment and ask them to look for similar evidence in older buildings or ancient sites.

■ Look for simple changes in homes, in school and in modern streets. It will help them discover changes more easily in past environments.

Ask the same questions about three different buildings.

■ Why are particular building materials used?

■ Does the shape of the building help us work out what it was used for?

■ Is there any evidence to suggest that it might be a new or old building?

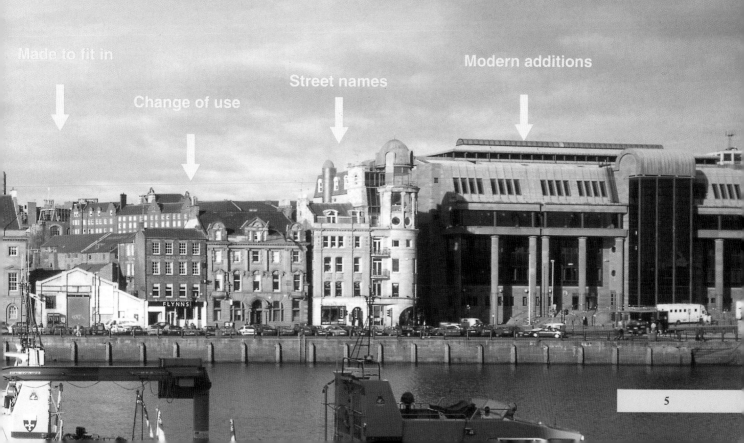

Made to fit in

Change of use

Street names

Modern additions

ASKING THE RIGHT QUESTIONS

By looking closely at a building and asking relevant questions you can encourage pupils to find out about it for themselves. There are five types of questions which can be used as a framework in examining the evidence. They are:

■ WHAT questions: what is this place for? What needs was this building designed to meet?

■ HOW questions: how was it built?

■ WHY questions: why was it built? Why was it built here?

■ WHEN questions: when was it built? When was it changed?

■ WHO questions: who built it? Who lived here?

What and how questions make a good starting point for any work on site. They require pupils to think about a building as a system, as a place people lived or worked or worshipped in and as a building designed to meet certain needs. Once the what and how questions have been investigated there will be lots of information to help in working out the who, when and why.

WHEN WAS IT BUILT?

Pupils can try to decide if they think a house is older or younger than the house they live in, or other houses in the town or village around them.

WHEN WAS IT CHANGED?

The shape of windows and doors is a good indication of the date of a building, but they are also the features which get most often updated. Houses are constantly being modified to meet new needs and new demands. Alterations can reflect a need for more space, more status, keeping up with fashion, or a change of use in the building. Changes in brick and stonework, lines of old arches and bricked up fireplaces or windows, new-looking pipes and different shaped windows can all provide valuable clues about changes which have taken place over time.

Use the photocopiable activity *Looking at change* and ask pupils to decide which of these houses came first, then try to put them all in chronological order.

Ask your pupils to look out for different building materials.

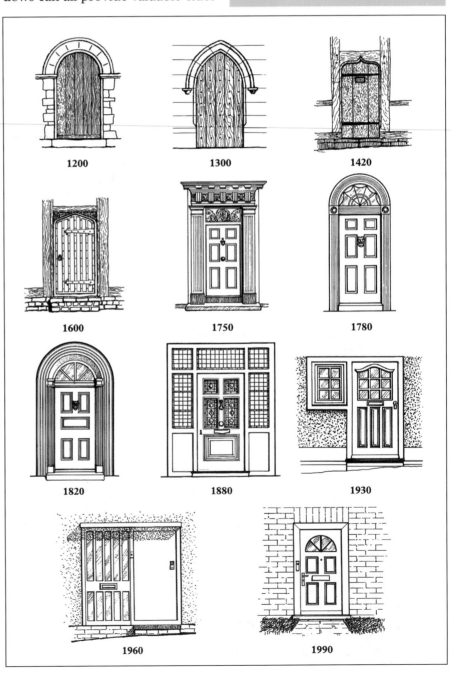

1200 1300 1420

1600 1750 1780

1820 1880 1930

1960 1990

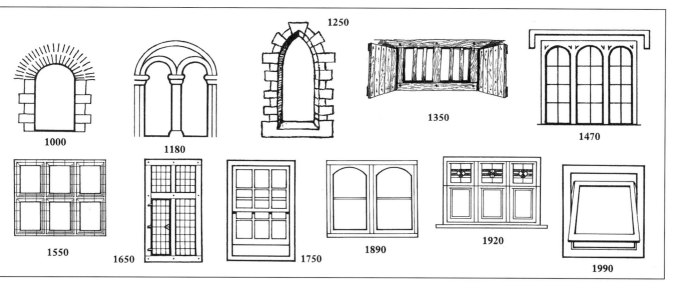

Georgian door with fanlight.

LEFT: *You will easily find a range of different doors and windows in any built-up area.*

RIGHT: *Classical influence continued to dominate more modest town houses until the Victorian period. These are in Hackney, London.*

Looking at change

Label the pictures of this house from 1 to 6 in date order

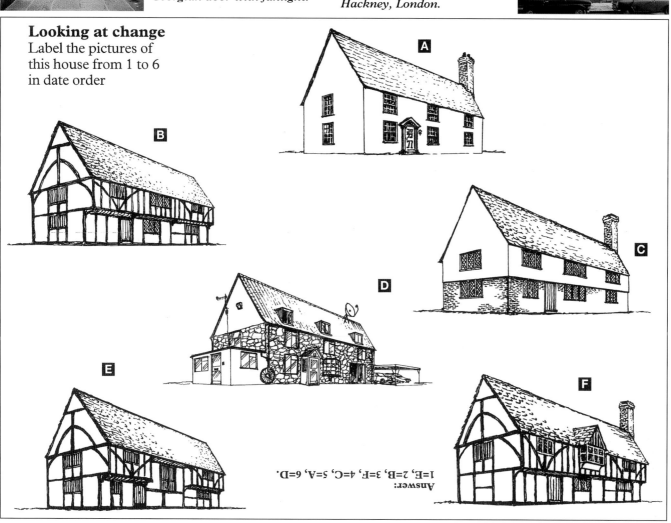

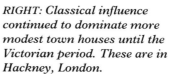

Answer:
1=E, 2=B, 3=F, 4=C, 5=A, 6=D.

ISSUES

Because we live in such a crowded place, it is inevitable that sometimes the old will have to give way to the new. The issues involved in choosing to preserve part of our past are complex but pupils should be encouraged to think about them. After all, they will need to live with the decisions made by us today. Just think of the problems we have to put up with today because of some 1960s' building designs!

Take these invented issues set out in a newspaper format (opposite), or find real ones from your own area. There are more ideas for dealing with issues of conservation, especially in newspapers, in Further reading and information.

Topics for issues could include:

War memorials

■ War memorials are still valued today by communities and many local people will still be related to those who died during the two World Wars.

■ Memorials were usually positioned so that they could be seen from a number of different points in the town or village, perhaps on an island at the meeting of three or more roads. Road patterns, and use, have changed enormously since the last war.

Churches

■ The parish church will often be the oldest building in the locality. Many are protected by law.

■ Any alteration or additions to protected buildings must receive consent and archaeological and survey work must be carried out in advance.

■ People often feel that ancient monument or historic building protection should not stand in the way of 'progress'.

Hospitals

■ Nineteenth-century hospitals were built to very different standards to those of today. Like schools of the same period, they are not necessarily easy to convert or adapt.

■ The building itself may be protected by law. If the health trust decides to sell the building, it may be saved by adapting it for other uses, such as flats.

Medieval bridges

■ A good example of an ancient monument with no practical use today.

■ However, it is an important landmark which people would not want to see destroyed.

■ Local examples of large sums of money being released by the Lottery for 'heritage' or arts projects could be discussed.

Pubs

■ Here there might be a question of whether we should replicate old buildings. Pubs are often places where 'old' things are displayed - for example, iron ploughs or antique ships' wheels - often quite out of context.

■ Do people really hate 'modern' buildings? Or are we afraid that the 'new' will not fit in with the 'old'?

■ Are we losing another part of our heritage when the names of pubs are changed? For example, from The Queen's Head to the Slug and Lettuce?

THE WEEKLY ECHO

Serving the people Friday April 1, 1999   32p

SAVE OUR HOSPITAL!

Local residents angry over closure plans

Residents in the Greenfields area of town today learnt of new health trust plans to close the emergency department of the hospital. Local campaigner, John Hoskyns said, "We knew that sooner or later the Trust would admit that our 100 year old hospital would close. When the emergency department goes, that'll be it". A Trust spokeswoman issued a statement which emphasised its commitment to providing local health care for local people, but admitted that maintaining an old building was too costly for them.

'IT'S AN OUTRAGE SAYS WAR VETERAN'

Bryan Magee, 85-year war veteran from the Alder Tree estate, was in blistering mood today after he found out that the roads department of the County Council were going to move the War Memorial. "My comrades are commemorated there as well as a generation before them who fell in the Great War. It's simply not right to dismantle it and put up a plaque in the town hall. I'm getting up a petition and I've got 30 signatures already." The War Memorial was put up after the First World War by public subscription and further names were added after 1945. The memorial was the work of a local firm, Cosby & Sons, formerly at Union Street (now the Co-op).

"WE NEED ROOM TO PRAY", SAYS LOCAL CONGREGATION

Local worshippers at St Margaret's, Great Blessingford, are hoping that their diocese will give permission for a new room to be added to their church. Churchwarden Jill

Hanratty said, "We know the church is very old but we must move with the times. We need better facilities like toilets and a room for nursing mothers if we are to attract a younger congregation". The county's archaeologists say the church's origins are Saxon and that it had been altered and added to in the 12th to 14th centuries.

DRINKERS FLEE BLAZING PUB

It wasn't 'Time gentlemen please' which landlord, Ken McVitie aged 28, shouted at about closing time on Saturday at the King's Head in Lambs Lane. He was shocked to discover a fire raging in the cellar and the pub had to be evacuated. The fire had taken hold even before the local fire service could reach the pub. The pub is one of the town's few historic buildings and was dated to 1765. Its timber structure has been almost entirely destroyed. Mr McVitie is determined to carry on though, "We will simply have to build a replica King's Head. My customers like to drink in familiar surroundings".

LOTTERY LOLLY FOR LOCAL LANDMARK
By our villages correspondent

Villagers at Great Brentley were overjoyed yesterday as news reached them that their bid for Lottery money had been successful. Now £167,000 will be available to repair the ancient medieval packhorse bridge which is the centre piece of their village. The bridge was closed to traffic in 1974 after dangerous cracks were discovered and a new bridge built. Repairs then were only £2,500 - the cost of maintaining ancient monuments has certainly risen since then!

INSIDE
Your pet could win a walking holiday for two along fabulous Hadrian's Wall

MY CLASS IS IN RUINS

Many teachers worry about visiting and using ruined sites - ancient monuments - with their classes. Some believe that the 'country house' is easier because it is full of things to see. In fact ruins, without the accumulated junk of the past, can often be more stimulating for pupils. It can make them think and use their imagination. It is also an opportunity to investigate interpretations that people in the present, and the recent past, have put on the remains.

Preparation is particularly important as pupils will not be used to seeing what is, essentially, a plan of a building with, perhaps, some walls surviving to roof height. You could use some of these ideas before you make a site visit:

■ Get your pupils to make a plan of their own

classroom. Make sure that they add the position of windows and, in particular, doors. They should plot in any features, such as built-in cupboards, sinks and radiators. Desks, worktops, bookcases and chairs should also be added.

■ Compare these with other plans, perhaps of ancient sites or buildings so that they are familiar with the idea.

Once on site you might use these ideas:

■ Ask your pupils to walk around the site themselves, perhaps working in pairs or small groups. Tell them that they must only enter rooms through the doorways - never walk over the walls. Ask them to try to make sense of what they are investigating. Where are the entrances? Are there any windows?

■ If you provide them with a plan of the site, they could identify other features, such as fireplaces or a water supply.

■ Get them to look for clues to upper floors which have long since gone - for example, holes for floor joists, fireplaces and windows set high in a wall and the remains of staircases.

■ Ask them to question the evidence they can see - for example, does a room with fine decoration, a grand fireplace and large windows tell us that it was for someone important? Do tiny slit-like windows, thick walls and stout entrances indicate a defensive structure?

■ Sometimes only the foundations of buildings survive. Explain what foundations are and look for modern ones in buildings being built now.

Back at school you might return to the plan they prepared of their classroom and ask them how an archaeologist of the future might interpret the remains. How did people get in and out? What was the room used for and by what sort of people?

ORGANISATION CHECKLIST
Always check that you have:

☐   made the purpose of the visit clear to all colleagues and helpers concerned

☐   confirmed all bookings in writing

☐   checked insurance cover

☐   completed a Risk Assessment form if required by your school or LEA

☐   obtained permission slips from all parents of pupils intending to go on the visit

☐   received enough voluntary contributions to cover the cost of the visit

☐   informed parents why the visit is taking place, what clothing pupils should wear, what time the coach is due back at school, what the lunch arrangements are and how much money (if any) their children might need

☐   booked the coach and checked times with the company

☐   organised adequate staff supervision/ratio

☐   informed other colleagues that you will be out of school on the day

☐   organised appropriate provision for any pupil with special needs

☐   gathered all the necessary equipment and first aid boxes

☐   compiled an accurate register of all pupils on the visit and that you have left a copy with the school secretary

☐   left emergency contact numbers for the site with the school secretary.

RESOURCES CHECKLIST
The following list contains basic requirements and would need to be amended in light of the planned on-site activities:

☐   clipboards (one per pupil)

☐   suitable paper for recording observations (A4 size)

☐   large drawing boards and paper (A3 size)

☐   writing/drawing equipment for each pupil (pencils are more useful than pens)

☐   measuring equipment

☐   a box of art equipment

☐   tape recorder(s)

☐   Polaroid or digital camera(s)

☐   video camcorder(s)

☐   plans of the site

☐   first aid box.

TAKE NOTE

How many times, on a visit to an historic site, have you said to your class something like 'Have a good look round and make a few notes on what you see'? But this can be a demanding task for many pupils, and the skill of note taking is too important to be left to chance.

DEVELOPING NOTE TAKING

One way to develop note taking is to encourage simple annotations of sketches made on site. In the drawing of Coalport Bridge, the Y5 pupil has used brief comments to augment observations on the structure of the bridge. Notice how technical, historical and personal information makes this a useful working document, not just a collection of random jottings. Simple annotations, too, could be made on photographs, perhaps Polaroids developed on site or added later in the classroom.

Initial sketches

The use of notes on initial sketches can be used in two ways. First, to provide prompts for further research back at school into, for example, when the building was constructed. Pupils might also think about whether all the sections were built at the same time

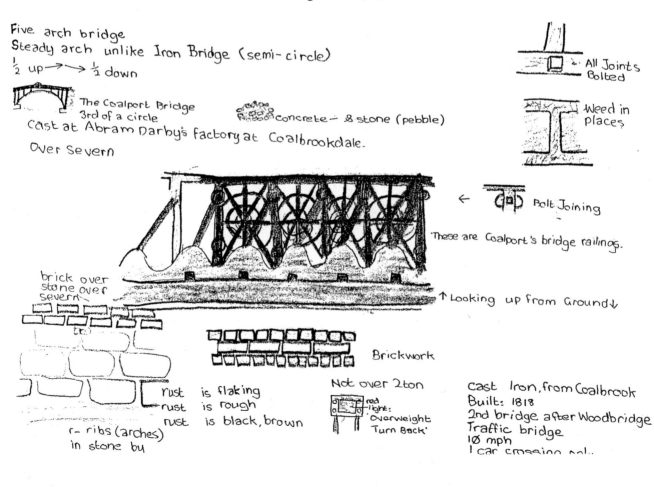

Coalport Bridge, Coalport.

Five arch bridge
Steady arch unlike Iron Bridge (semi-circle)
½ up ⟶ ½ down

The Coalport Bridge
3rd of a circle
Cast at Abram Darby's factory at Coalbrookdale.
Over Severn

concrete - & stone (pebble)

All Joints Bolted

Weed in places

Bolt Joining

These are Coalport's bridge railings.

↑ Looking up from Ground↓

brick over
stone over
Severn

Brickwork

rust is flaking
rust is rough
rust is black, brown

r- ribs (arches)
in stone by

Not over 2ton
red light:
'Overweight
Turn Back'

Cast Iron, from Coalbrook
Built: 1818
2nd bridge after Woodbridge
Traffic bridge
10 mph
1 car crossing only

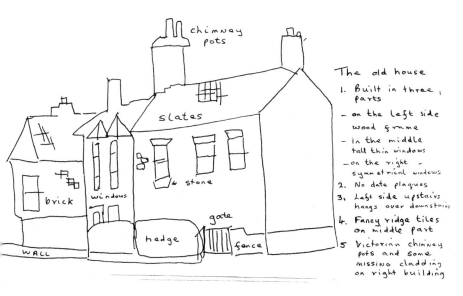

The old house
1. Built in three parts
  - on the left side wood frame
  - in the middle tall thin windows
  - on the right - symmetrical windows
2. No date plaques
3. Left side upstairs hangs over downstairs
4. Fancy ridge tiles on middle part
5. Victorian chimney pots and some missing cladding on right building

and why different materials were used for different sections. Second, to provide working notes for a more detailed and revised sketch as part of communicating history in a variety of ways.

MAKING OBSERVATIONS

Another strategy is to encourage limited observation. In the open-ended activity sheet for a visit to Harlech Castle, the pupil has been confined to three observations. Notice, too, how this Y6 historian is beginning to make guesses and pose further questions. She used further resources as the visit developed to answer some of her own questions.

PRE-VISIT PREPARATION

There are useful activities that can be done in school prior to any visit that will encourage successful note taking. These need not be related to the planned visit but will begin to develop the skills of note taking and annotating a sketch. For example:

■ give small groups of pupils an old artefact or object and ask them to write five words that describe what they see

■ extend this activity by passing the objects around and asking for one or two short sentences

■ give pupils a short piece of historical narrative, for example a suitable news item from last week's local paper. Ask them to use a highlighter to pick out the significant words. You could extend this activity to writing three key sentences that summarise the item.

OTHER RECORDING METHODS

There are, of course, other ways that pupils can record their observations. Many schools now have an increasingly sophisticated range of equipment - from audio and video recorders to digital cameras. You could also try producing specially-designed activity sheets or problem-solving scenarios.

Note taking, however, remains the simplest and cheapest key skill to teach and to use.

There were probably domestic lean-to buildings against the walls inside the central area. The marks on the walls are similar to those at Shrewsbury castle which I studied last year.

The land towards the sea is very flat. Perhaps the sea has pulled back. did it once came to the bottom of the rocky base of the castle?

Alan Sorrell's original painting is on the right as you enter the castle. Many of the things we guessed first of all seem to be true. The sea did come up to the walls! There was an entry port (Watergate) where ships could unload passengers and cargo. The castle dominated the town. Even today the town buildings seem to huddle under its shadow.

RECORDING GRAVESTONES

Whether your school is in an urban or rural area, it will not be very far away from a churchyard or municipal cemetery. Here you will find an exciting source of real historical evidence to examine, record and analyse. The most striking aspect of graveyards in this

country is the number of memorials inside a relatively small space - perhaps as many as 20 million survive in this country today. You might find some medieval memorials in your nearest church or churchyard, but you are more likely to see grave-stones from the eighteenth and nineteenth centuries.

SYMBOLISM

Symbols in carvings or statues are often used on memorials to convey a message about attitudes to death, as these examples show.

skull & crossed bones

mortality

hour glass/scythe

time/life has passed

angel

clasped hands

farewell

guardian (often with hands pointing towards heaven)

MAKING A RECORDING

Recording the information is important, and real, historical work which your pupils can do. You could use a specially-designed recording form (see page 70) but they should, at least, be recording the following information:

- inscription
- any decoration
- shape of memorial
- condition of memorial
- type(s) of material used.

Try recording grave-stones and memorials with a still or video camera.

ANALYSING THE DATA

A whole wealth of data can be collected from graveyard memorials which you can analyse back at school, for example:

■ by putting the gravestones in chronological order and seeing how decoration and inscriptions vary from century to century

■ by showing the periods when some parts of the graveyard were used

■ by drawing family trees from inscriptions

■ by investigating mortality statistics (for example, the age at death of all males)

■ by making a graph of the most popular first names of people who died during a specific period (for example, from 1850-1950).

IMPORTANT

Always get permission to take your class to visit and record the gravestones in a churchyard. You will need to be especially careful about going into areas:

■ where burials still take place

■ where graves have regular visitors

■ which have been set aside for wild plants.

Gravestones often have lichen growing on them. Do not allow your pupils to rub it off to read the inscription. Careful observation, and sometimes glancing light, will usually allow worn or obscured inscriptions to be read.

AN OBJECT LESSON

WHY USE OBJECTS?

Don't you just hate those museums or country houses which make it plain to you, the teacher, that your class shouldn't even think of touching anything! Of course, there will be very good reasons why some objects, and even some buildings, should be kept behind barriers. But people like to touch things. You can only learn a certain amount by observation. Objects (even replicas) brought into the classroom may help you motivate pupils more than the written word or discussion. 'Things' being handled by pupils will usually spark an interest, then curiosity which you can channel into further research.

DEVELOPING SKILLS

Handling objects will help your pupils develop a number of skills including:

- handling and observing
- comparing, deducing and evaluating
- recognising and identifying
- expressing themselves clearly
- classifying
- recording and presenting.

Asking questions

Get your pupils to ask questions of the objects, perhaps using the chart opposite. You could encourage your pupils to devise their own questions. The question you should never start with is 'What is it?' or 'What is the name for this?'. This question will simply close down other observations and deductions.

Close observation

A good way to develop close observation is to start with a familiar object. It might be a piece of classroom furniture, such as a chair, or something smaller, such as a pencil. You could talk your pupils through the observation and deduction stages. Use other objects or constructions in the classroom to reinforce deductions. For example, if they conclude that the chair is made of wood, look for other examples of the materials which surround them and you.

Think about asking older members of your community to talk with your pupils about objects they once used.

RECORDING

Close observation can be accompanied by recording. Think about using a number of techniques to suit your own pupils, for example:

- **careful drawing from different angles**

How many drawings might one object need to explain to others what it was like?

- **written description**

Ask your pupils to think carefully about the words they use. What is big to one person, is quite different to another.

- **tape-recorded or video-taped description**

Alternative methods of recording may help pupils to develop literary skills.

LOOKING AT AN OBJECT

The main things to think about	Some further questions to ask	Things found out by looking	Things to be researched
WHAT DOES IT LOOK AND FEEL LIKE?	Colour? Smell? Sound? Made of? Natural or manufactured? Complete? Changed/mended? Worn?		
HOW WAS IT MADE?	By hand? By machine? Fixed together by what?		
WHAT WAS IT MADE FOR?	Used for? Has the use changed?		
IS IT WELL DESIGNED?	Does it do its job? Made of the best materials? Decorated? How decorated? Like the look of it? Would others like the look of it?		
WHAT IS IT WORTH?	To those who made it? To those who used it? To you? To a museum?		

THE MYSTERY OBJECT

One good way of encouraging observation and deduction is to provide pupils with a mystery object. It is not always easy to find something which no pupil will have seen before. Few modern items will work (although almost no pupils in urban schools will recognize a clay pigeon!). Some objects from the last war or from the Victorian period will usually suffice.

I've never seen one of these before

It looks old and worn

The idea of the 'mystery object' is to take away the knowledge of what it is (what it is called). This helps pupils concentrate on thinking careful-ly and reaching conclusions based on the evidence they hold in their hands.

What is it made of?

Which way up does it go?   *What does it do?*

(A STONE HOT WATER BOTTLE.)

OBJECT GAMES

LEARNING FROM FRAGMENTS

It is one thing to use whole objects in the classroom. It is quite another to ask pupils to cope with fragments of objects. Archaeologists work mostly from fragments - pieces of broken bone, bits of pottery, discarded building materials. They usually only find a fragment of what once formed the whole picture. Many things rot away or are re-used in a completely different situation. Here are some games to play with your class to help them look at evidence.

KEY STAGE IDEAS

At KS1

■ Play the 'Feely Bag Game'. Put an object in a cloth bag or pillow case. Ask one pupil to put her hands inside and describe to the others what she can feel - but without giving it a name. The others have to guess what the hidden object is.
  You could start with familiar objects and move onto historic ones.

At KS 2

■ Play the 'Left Luggage Game'. Put a number of objects inside a suitcase. Ask a group of pupils to investigate each object and try to work out what sort of person owned the suitcase and its objects. Do the contents indicate where he (or is it a she) was going to, or was he coming from somewhere?

THE SKELETON GAME

Ask one of your class to 'play dead'. Tell them '*This is ....*
What can we find out about ....?
But we can't ask her any questions.
We have to figure out what kind of person she is only from what she is wearing and carrying.

Let's imagine........has been buried for about 2000 years. What will be left of .... and what she is wearing and carrying?' You can then discuss the difficulties of building up a picture from slender evidence.

THE POTATO GAME.

Give each pupil in a group a potato (or you could equally use an apple) and ask them to write down a detailed description so that other members of the group cannot see what they have written. When they have finished, collect the potatoes and put them in the centre. Pupils must find the right potato as the descriptions are read out. Alternatively, this exercise can be done by drawn rather than written descriptions.

Pupils playing the 'Left Luggage Game'.

THE DUSTBIN GAME

Here is a photograph of a 'slice through' a real dustbin. You could easily produce similar evidence by tipping out the clasroom's waste paper basket after a day's use. There are two routes you can guide your class along:

Route 1

Archaeologists are like police detectives - looking for the smallest clues to help them find out what happened in the past. What does this rubbish tell us about the people who threw it away? Ask pupils to give the evidence to answer questions such as

■ Are there any children in this family?

■ What kinds of food do they eat?

■ Do they have any pets?

■ What sort of pets and how many?

■ What season of the year is it? Are they Easter eggs wrappers or bits of Christmas decorations?

Ask your pupils if the dustbin rubbish can tell us anything else.

Route 2

In the past, people got rid of their rubbish wherever they could - they dug pits, threw it into ditches, filled hollows in the landscape, used old wells and spread it on fields. Let's imagine that this dustbin-full has been buried somewhere. After some time (depending on soil conditions) quite a lot of it will have rotted away. Organic material (that is, things which were once living such as paper or wood) will tend to rot quicker than inorganic things (that is, things which were never 'alive', such as plastic or metal).

The large dark areas here are rubbish pits exposed by archaeologists at the Saxon settlement of West Heslerton (see page 42).

TASK

Ask pupils to work out what the archaeologist might be left with after all the organic material had rotted away. How difficult might it be, then, to reach conclusions about the people who threw this rubbish away?

EVIDENCE FROM DOCUMENTS

WHAT ARE DOCUMENTS?

Documentary evidence comes in many different forms - from hand-written parchments to photographs. Though all documents are important evidence for studying the past, only some are stored securely in record offices (see below). You will find many interesting and useful sources in your own locality.

TYPES OF DOCUMENTS

The list of documents below is by no means exhaustive but does include the most useful for studying people and places with pupils.

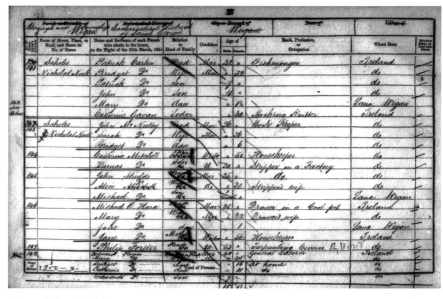

Part of the 1851 Census.

Census records were first collected in 1801 and a similar exercise has been carried out every ten years since then (with the exception of 1941). From 1841 the information collected was more precise.

Parish registers were introduced to record the main events in the lives of Christians - births and baptisms, marriages and burials - and were kept (in theory) in each parish from 1538 onwards.

Maps exist for some sections of the country from the medieval period. Maps of estates become more common from the sixteenth century. Maps were drawn up under the Enclosure Acts of the eighteenth and nineteenth centuries. The Ordnance Survey began to map the whole country on a scale of 1 inch to 1 mile from the beginning of the nineteenth century. Tithe maps and accompa-

nying documents, called awards, were drawn up for most places between 1836 and 1850 to work out how much each landowner or tenant owed the church in tithe.

Photographs exist in large numbers from the nineteenth century onwards. They can catch the mood of the time and provide invaluable evidence for events, people and places.

Estate map of Goddard's Farm, Thaxted, Essex 1706.

Victorian store in Byfield, Northamptonshire.

Local directories

Trades or Post Office directories were like the Yellow Pages of the nineteenth century. They provide a wealth of information, for example, lists of householders, trades and shops, important buildings and communication routes. These examples come from *Kelly's Directory of Essex, 1895.*

ABBOT'S ROOTHING.

Cure Rev. Lawrence Capel B.A. Rctry
Rattee Rev. James E. (Congregatnl)
Barker Thos. S. frmr. Berwick's frm

Blowes John, beer retailer & carrier
Kinsey James, farmer, Nether street
Metson Jacob, farmer, Parker's farm

Parmenter Mary (Mrs.), Anchor P.H
Thurgood James, farmer, Rookwoods & Abbot's halls

AYTHROP ROOTHING.

Ludgater Rev. Henry M.A. Rectory
COMMERCIAL.
Aldham Thomas Allaker, farmer & landowner, Highams
Aylett Elizabeth (Miss), Carpenters' Arms P.H

Aylett John, beer retailer
Belsham Thos. miller (wind & steam)
Blyth Charles, farm bailiff to Mr. John Gingell, Friar's grange
Caton W. Draper, farmer
Clayden Thomas, grocer & draper

Dunmow John, farmer, Cut Elms
Livermore Charles, jun. farmer, Aythrop hall
Matthams James Barnard, farmer
Shead Mary Ann (Mrs.), blacksmith
Stokes William, farmer, Keers

BEAUCHAMP ROOTHING.

Clay Lieut.-Col. Albert Newby J.P. Slades
Howard Rev. John B.A. Rectory
COMMERCIAL.
Blowes John Parker, shopkeeper, Butt hatch

Elliott Alfred, farmer
Hammond Arthur, builder
Horsnell Geo. shopkeeper, Birds green
Newman George, farmer, Long Barnes
Speller Elizabeth (Mrs.), Swan inn, Birds green

Read James, farmer, Butt hatch
Walden Joseph, farmer, Willie's farm
Warder Nathan, farm bailiff to Messrs. Duffield & Bruity, Wood end
Whitbread Hy. beer ret. Birds green

PARKESTON QUAY, formed by the Great Eastern Railway Co. and opened for traffic in 1883, is situated upon the Stour, 2½ miles up the river, and was constructed for developing their Continental traffic. This quay, with station and loop line, occupied four years in construction, and cost about £500,000. Although a little higher up the river than the old pier, there is a saving of time in starting from Parkeston quay, on account of the clearer course, and consequently the boat train leaves London later than hitherto. About 600 acres of land have been acquired by the company, the greater portion reclaimed from the bed of the river, by a curved embankment 2½ miles long; in the centre of the curve is the quay, 1,800 feet long, affording berths for seven vessels, while seven more can be moored in the river. The quay wall is formed by screw piles, those in front being 2 feet in diameter, and those at the back being 1 foot 6 in.; between them are concrete cylinders of seven rings each, and 9 feet in outside diameter, sunk in pairs. On the quay are two goods warehouses, each 520 feet long by 100 feet wide. A passenger gangway 40 feet wide leads to the central building of 350 feet frontage, which serves for the station and hotel. All the buildings and platforms are erected upon piles, of which there are more than 1,000, sunk to the ancient bed of the river.

The church of St. Nicholas is a structure of white brick in the debased Perpendicular style, consisting of chancel, nave, aisles and an embattled western tower, with pinnacles and spire, containing a clock and 8 bells : it was rebuilt and enlarged in 1821 by subscription and a rate: there are three partially-stained windows in the chancel, and in the vestry is a tablet containing the names of the vicars of this church from 1336 to 1874: there are 1,500 sittings, of which 1,000 are free. The register dates from the year 1550. The living is a vicarage, average tithe rent-charge £45, net yearly value £51, in the gift of J. E. A. Gwynne esq. F.S.A. of Folkington manor, Polegate, Sussex.

St. Nicholas Mission room, Bathside, erected in May, 1879, is a wooden building, and will seat 40 persons.

There is an iron Mission church at Parkeston, seating about 100 persons.

Grafton (The) Fur Company Limited
164 New Bond street, London W
The leading house for furs in London

International Fur Store

Trade Mark.
163 & 198 Regent street W. The largest stock of furs of any house in London

Household removals

FINDING THE RECORDS

Documents can be found in local or county record offices and in local study sections of public libraries.

■ Always work out in advance how you want to use documents as part of your curriculum work.

■ Go and see what records and facilities are available.

■ Ask if the office or library has an education officer or special school packs.

■ Try the internet to access local archive information.

GREAT OAKLEY is a village and parish, on Ramsey Creek, a feeder of the Stour, and on the road from Colchester to Harwich, 5 miles north from Thorpe-le-Soken station on the Colchester and Walton-on-the-Naze line, and 4 south from Wrabness station on the Harwich and Manningtree branch of the Great Eastern railway, 6 south-west from Harwich, 7 south-east from Manningtree, 14 from Colchester and 65 from London, in the North Eastern division of the county, hundred, petty sessional division and union of Tendring, Harwich county court district and in the rural deanery of Ardleigh and Harwich, archdeaconry of Colchester and diocese of St. Albans. The church of All Saints is an ancient building of stone and brick, partly Norman and consisting of chancel and nave and a belfry containing one bell : in the nave is a tablet to the Rev. Richard Drake M.A. rector here 1718, who erected an almshouse for four aged women of the parish : there is a fine Norman font of polished marble, supported on five stone shafts : the church was restored in 1880, w] **21** moved and the pews replaced by open benches at a cost of £400, defrayed by general contributions; during the

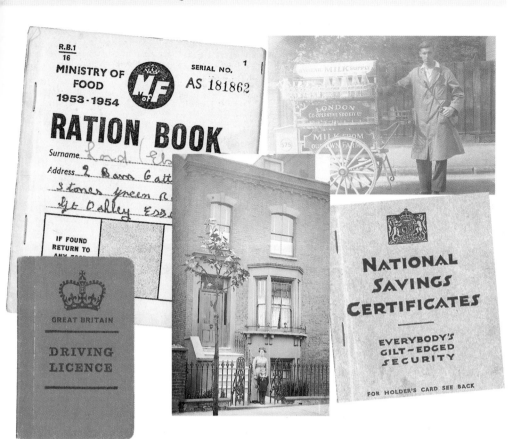

COMMUNITY RECORDS

Sources of documentary evidence are easy to collect from parents, governors and friends. Most people have records of their families going back at least one generation. Some of the most common are illustrated here.

School records

If you are lucky your school will have records stored there. If not you should enquire at your nearest record office. Look out for:

Log books The principal teacher had to make an entry at least once a week. You will find information about a variety of subjects such as attendance, punishments, national events, weather, illness and pupils' achievements.

School closes this afternoon, for organised picking of Blackberries, in accordance with Board of Education Circular 1056. — 1918

Av. att. Mixed = 79.4   Infants = 30.1
Gerald & Joyce Gladwell are excluded owing to Ringworm. — 1919

Owing to parts of ceiling having given way, with consequent danger to children, School closes this afternoon, for repairs. — 1921

Nurse Wallace called with reference to Dorothy Wrycraft, excluded on 3 March, verminous — still in the same state this morning — sent home by School Nurse, again. — 1922

For dinner today only boiled potatoes & rice arrived. — 1944

School did not meet today — being the occasion of the cessation of hostilities in Europe. — 1945

School log book entries.

KEY STAGE IDEAS

At KS1
■ Use a collection of old photographs of people and buildings with photographs of surroundings which are familiar to them (family, school, locality) and ask pupils to look for differences (such as clothes, hairstyles, cars) and similarities (buildings unchanged, postboxes).

■ Use the photographs to extend their ideas about modern, old, very old, very very old by gradually introducing them to changes such as fashion.

■ Introduce them to the idea of documents by comparing present-day documents (such as bus pass, passport, credit card, supermarket till receipt, train ticket) with older documents in the original or facsimile (such as shop receipt, old bus/train ticket, ration book).

At KS 2
■ Use a modern map/street plan to plot which parts of their local surroundings still exist and which are now missing or have been changed. Compare with older maps from the local studies collection.

■ Use old photographs to look for the number of changes which have taken place, for example fashions, technology, different building materials, words and styles used for shop or industry advertisements.

■ Using one or two examples, look at the way language has changed in documents. For example, compare the words used to describe a business in a post office directory with the way a similar business is described in the Yellow Pages.

AN EYE FOR DETAIL

Photographs are an easy historical source to come by. Most towns and many villages have books of old photos published about them. Your local record office, museum or library will have collections. You can find them in old newspapers as well. You could also make your own collection. Look out for postcards in book or antique shops, but don't forget to ask parents of your pupils or other people in your area.

WHAT'S GOING ON HERE?

This photo (RIGHT) was taken c1903. It shows the bandstand built in 1889 when Clacton had a resident German band as well as visiting regimental military bands. You could enlarge this picture and ask pupils to think about the following, perhaps using a magnifying glass:

■ what are the clues which indicate that the sea is in front of this picture (man with binoculars, children looking over fence, people sitting in deckchairs facing that way, glass panels around the bandstand to keep the wind off?)

■ the sorts of clothes people are wearing (how many types of hats?). Compare these with what people would wear today at the seaside.

■ there is a pram and a pushchair. How do they differ from ones in use today?

You might follow up by looking at documentary evidence. The census and ticket returns show the popularity of Clacton on Sea:

Census 1891: 651
Census 1901: 7,456
Pier tickets 1883: 92,873
Pier tickets 1893: 327,450

The Bandstand, Clacton on Sea.

SPOTTING CHANGES

These two photographs (BELOW) are of Exeter, Devon, taken 42 years apart. They are from English Heritage's National Monuments Record. You could ask your pupils to look out and discuss:

■ **changes over time**. For example, the 1946 photograph shows areas of bomb damage which have been filled in by 1988.

■ **land use**. For example, areas close to the river were used for industry in 1946 but had been redeveloped for housing by 1988.

■ **new roads**. For example, while some main roads have survived on the 1988 photograph, it is clear that Exeter now has a major inner city road system with roundabouts, flyovers and bridges.

1946

1988

INTERPRETING HISTORY

Different types of interpretation for the visitor at Hailes Abbey, Gloucestershire.

"There is no such thing as a fact in history". Discuss.

This might be a good starting point for you to begin thinking about how to teach interpretation of history. Everything you see, hear or read has been presented to us through an interpreter. The interpreter might be

■ an historian reading a manuscript and giving a view of what it means

■ an archaeologist analysing the

results of an excavation or a survey of a landscape and publishing a report of what it appears to mean

■ a restorer of the physical fabric of an historic site who draws on evidence from elsewhere to re-create what a building might have looked like

■ an interpreter or writer who presents a story of what a particular part of the past seems to be, through displays, exhibitions, guidebooks, guided tours or re-enactments.

In some places the interpretation can be in the form of actual reconstruction. You can see examples on pages 48-49 from The Jorvik Viking Centre. This physical

The main gate to the Roman fort at Saalburg, Germany.

reconstruction of part of a Roman fort in Germany was based on excavation of the site. Archaeologists and Roman historians can argue about whether it is a 'correct' reconstruction but at least it provides the visitor with an impression of what it might have been like here in Roman times.

Re-enactors from the Ermine Street Guard group at Wroxeter Roman City, Shropshire.

The refectory at Rievaulx Abbey, North Yorkshire with an artist's impression. How much is based on the evidence seen on site and how much has been left to the artist's own interpretation?

ARTISTS' IMPRESSIONS

Many historic sites and museums use artists' impressions of what a place or an object or an event might have looked like in the past. They are probably the most readily accessible resource for both classroom and on-site use (see page 71 for further information). They are particularly useful for site visits because:

■ they recreate missing parts of a site to help pupils to understand about life in the past

■ they can be used as an example of the way in which the past is interpreted

■ they provide an additional type of visual source to supplement photographs, paintings or illustrated manuscripts

■ they allow pupils to identify aspects of the site which have remained unchanged (continuity) and those parts which have been altered (change)

■ they help teachers show how a building might have looked at a particular point in its history

■ they provide an accessible resource not dependent on a pupil's reading ability.

Part of the museum display at Avebury, Wiltshire.

ONLY HALF THE STORY?

The photograph above shows how English Heritage tried to encourage visitors to the museum at Avebury Stone Circle to think about evidence and how it might be interpreted. The museum exhibition and displays tell the story of the circle, something about life at the time and how the circle was excavated in the 1920s and 1930s.

This full size Neolithic figure was deliberately dressed in two halves:

■ the half on the right shows a rather raggedly-dressed man coping with his existence. The clothes are dull and are based on surviving evidence.

■ the other half on the left shows a much more colourful figure. His body is painted and tattooed and his clothes are much better made and has different types of jewellery attached.

The two halves represent the extremes of interpretation in two respects. First they represent some people's view that prehistoric people lived dull, rather barbaric lives while others that prehistoric people at this time were generally quite sophisticated - or they would not have been able to create a society which produced amazing monuments such as Avebury and Stonehenge. Second, the 'dull' half is based purely on surviving evidence from fragments of fabric from graves, while the 'colourful' half uses evidence from elsewhere in Neolithic Britain (and Europe) where tattooed skin and beautifully-made jewellery has survived.

The siege of Dover Castle by the French in 1216 dramatically presented in an artist's impression.

Kenilworth Castle, Warwickshire. The castle today seen from the air and an artist's impression of what it might have been like in the Elizabethan period.

CASE STUDY	AN ANGLO-SAXON HERMITAGE

HISTORICAL BACKGROUND

Lindisfarne Priory was founded in 635 by Aidan, a monk from the island monastery of Iona in south-west Scotland. King Oswald had invited him to convert his kingdom of Northumbria to Christianity.

The island site provided a degree of seclusion for the monks, to which they had been accustomed on Iona, while being easily accessible from the mainland and under the protection the royal fortress of Bamburgh six miles away.

The Priory's most famous inhabitant in the seventh century was Cuthbert, who later became Bishop of Lindisfarne from 685-7. He was noted for his travels to preach to the north's scattered communities, his desire to live a solitary life on St Cuthbert's Island and the island of Inner Farne (both are close to Lindisfarne), his affinity with birds and animals and his miracles of healing. After his death, Cuthbert was canonised and his grave became the focus of pilgrimages, one of the most important centres of Christianity in Anglo-Saxon England.

THE TASK

English Heritage, the guardians of Lindisfarne Priory, wanted to show the public, in guidebooks and exhibition displays, what St Cuthbert's hermitage on the island of Inner Farne may have looked like in the late seventh century AD. The medium chosen was an artist's painting. The painter chosen was Peter Dunn, a reconstruction artist employed by English Heritage.

THE PROCESS

Peter used a number of sources to complete the reconstruction:

■ the remains of the site itself on Inner Farne

■ documentary evidence, both primary sources (such as the Venerable Bede's *Ecclesiastical History of the English People* and *Life of Cuthbert*) and secondary sources (such as archaeological or historical investigations).

■ photographs, plans and maps

■ information and opinion from archaeologists and historians.

Later Cuthbert.... entered upon the contemplative life of a hermit in silent retreat from the world. Now it was a place utterly barren of water, corn or trees, and unsuitable besides for human habitation because frequented by evil spirits. After driving out these enemies he built for himself on the island with the help of the brothers a small dwelling, containing only the essential buildings, an oratory and a communal living-room surrounded by an earthwork.

Bede, after visiting the island around 721.

Stage I

The first stage was to use the most accessible sources to produce a rough sketch. The finished painting had to be based on real evi-

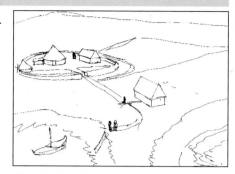

Rough sketch to show layout of the buildings on Inner Farne.

dence, of course, but it also had to suit its final use. An aerial view was thought best because it would more easily allow the visitors to get an idea of what the whole island may have looked like in Cuthbert's time.

The various sources of evidence suggested that there was a landing place, a guesthouse and an enclosure with several buildings.

Stage 2

This stage included three detailed sketches which were gradually altered as archaeologists compared Peter's drawing with the available evidence and their own knowledge. The example below incorporated some of the questions asked by Peter and comments from the archaeologists.

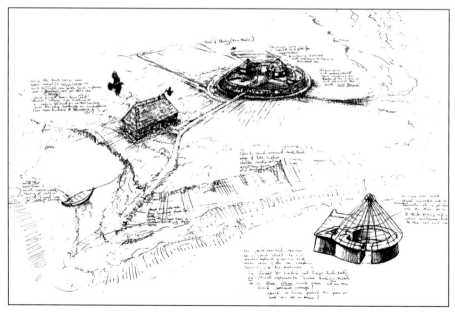

Second stage drawing with notes.

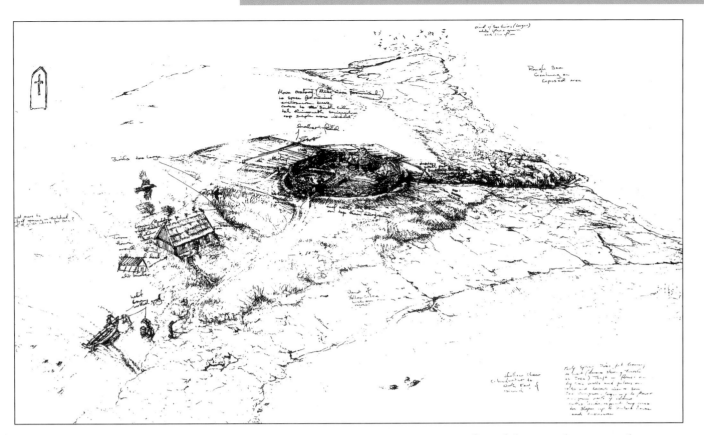

One of the second stage roughs.

Stage 3

The final stage was to complete the reconstruction in colour, incorporating all the latest comments. At this stage Peter had to ensure that the right colours were being used for the natural surroundings of the hermitage (the rock formations, for example) as well as for the construction materials.

Peter Dunn's reconstruction painting of St Cuthbert's hermitage on Inner Farne as it might have appeared in the late seventh century AD.

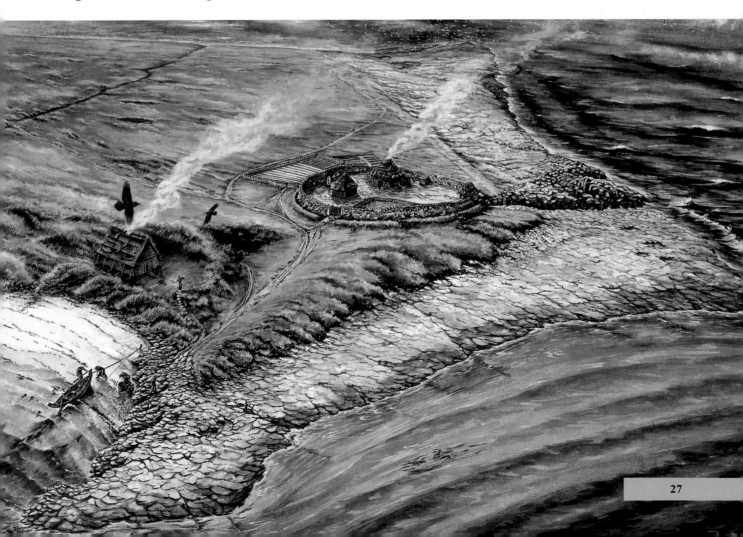

ACTIVITY SHEET

FABULOUS FRONTS

The next time you are walking down your local street, look at the fronts of the buildings. Then look up. Buildings are not just built simply of brick, stone or concrete. You will be very surprised at how much decoration will catch your eye.

   Why do buildings have decoration on them? To help you work out the reasons, tick the boxes below these pictures. A word of warning though! There is no single answer and there could be other reasons which you could add yourself.

❑ *impress people going inside*
❑ *remind the owner of other parts of the world*
❑ *show off the latest style*

❑ *be decorative*
❑ *advertise a company*
❑ *show off craft skills*

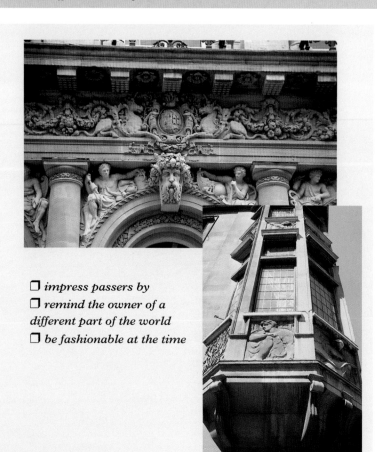

❑ *impress passers by*
❑ *remind the owner of a different part of the world*
❑ *be fashionable at the time*

❑ *stand out from other buildings*
❑ *advertise a company*
❑ *show off craft skills*

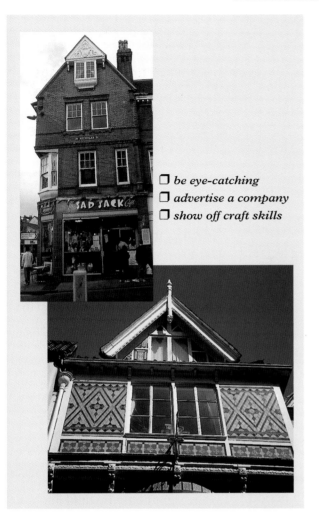

- ❏ *be eye-catching*
- ❏ *advertise a company*
- ❏ *show off craft skills*

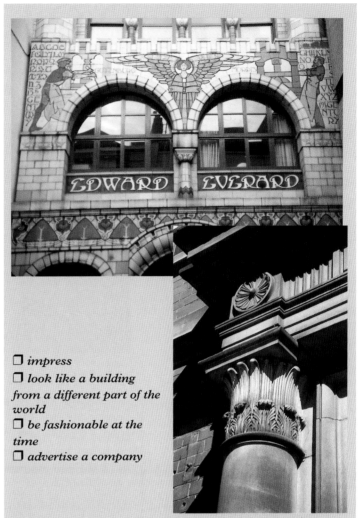

- ❏ *impress*
- ❏ *look like a building from a different part of the world*
- ❏ *be fashionable at the time*
- ❏ *advertise a company*

- ❏ *show what went on inside*
- ❏ *use mass-produced decorative materials*
- ❏ *show that the owner was rich and very educated*

- ❏ *impress*
- ❏ *use mass-produced decorative materials*
- ❏ *pretend to be a very posh building*

LOOKING AT HOUSES

Key Stage 1 children already know a lot about houses from their own direct experience and from stories. You can build on this to explore how people lived beyond our memories, by using the stepping stones of similarities and differences. Start by asking your class for all the things that go to build up a house - walls, roof, windows, doors. Then explore what there might be inside.

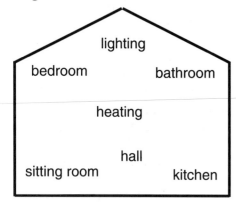

Now ask for the differences in types of dwellings:

- flats
- terraced houses
- detached houses
- semi-detached houses
- bungalows
- caravans
- bedsits.

Point out that although they are all very different, they all have in common most of the things outlined in your first lists. In the same way houses in the past look very different, but all have most of the facilities that we still need today. Use the pictures on the following pages to make the point.

NOW AND THEN

Use the different features on the *Now*, *Long Ago* and *Very Long Ago* (pages 32-34) as a hook to hang on snippets of information about the time. For example, windows in the modern and Victorian period are different in design but both are large because glass could be produced cheaply and in large sheets, but in medieval times glass was produced by hand and was so valuable that only rich people could afford it, and they took it with them when they moved house. As a result, most people had glassless windows, protected by wooden shutters or bars.

Similarly, lighting has changed over time. In the medieval period, beeswax candles were used by the rich, and the poor had foul-smelling tallow ones or rushes dipped in mutton fat. All created a smoky atmosphere. The Victorians had firstly oil lamps, then gas light, and now there is clean, very bright, electric light. A good way to show pupils at first hand the dim, flickering lighting available in medieval times is to bring a candle into school and light it in a darkened classroom (check smoke alarm tolerance first!).

You can take comparisons further using your own research with the pupils. For example, how clothes were washed, or floors cleaned.

Sorting it out

Use the pictures at the bottom of the *Now*, *Long Ago* and *Very Long Ago* pages for recognition and classification exercises: photocopy the pages, cut the bottom strips off omitting the caption, and cut into individual features, then ask pupils to put them into groups according to function, or match them up with the features in the big pictures. Two sets of features, lavatories and cooking places, have been added which are not in the main pictures: see if your pupils can assign these to the right house by thinking about the technology or decorative taste involved. Keep the captions if you want to use these as word recognition exercises as well.

Finding out

Enlist the help of parents and grandparents and ask for objects from a 1950s' house. See if you can find one near school to look at, even if it is just from the outside. Pupils can create a collage of a 1950s' house from their own sketches of the real thing, or copied from books, or by collecting pictures from magazines. They can be presented in the same format as the pictures in this book, and displayed on the wall or as information to accompany a class museum. Better still, ask a grandparent to come in and talk about what daily life was like then.

Visits

If you go to visit an old house, use the picture of the modern house and its features as a checklist, discovering similarities and differences. Alternatively, cut down on distractions and home in on just one feature and examine it really closely, like the cooking arrangements or the lighting, the windows, or the furniture.

CROSS CURRICULAR

Incorporate other subjects into your investigation of houses. Read the story of *The Three Little Pigs* in the Literacy Hour to introduce the idea that houses need to be made from appropriate materials. Follow this up by bringing some straw, twigs and a brick into school and leaving them outside for a couple of days to see what happens to them.

Look at the houses in the immediate vicinity of the school to see what they are made of, and use potato prints to make pictures of them back in class. If you visit an unfurnished house, pace out the size of the rooms, then get pupils to do the same to their own living rooms and compare the differences.

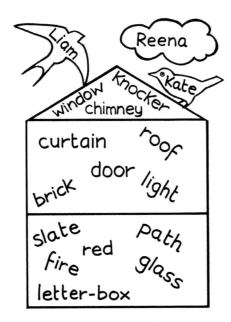

Draw a stylised picture of a square house with a triangular roof, rectangular windows and a door with a circular door knob, then ask pupils how many of these shapes they can see on their way to school, or on a walk in the area.

Ask pupils for words to describe the different features in the pictures of the three different houses in this book, like wall, door, bed, roof, and bring in comparative words, like bigger and biggest. Enter the words you want them to know in a huge outline on the classroom wall of a house with a downstairs, upstairs and attic; classify the words first into easy (downstairs), less easy (upstairs) and hard (attic). When pupils can spell all the words downstairs, they can move upstairs, and after that the attic, adding in their own names above the roof.

Use the Literacy Hour to read stories about how people lived, and what they ate. Make up a story about a child losing something in one of the houses in this book, and get your pupils to develop it by thinking of places where the object might be hidden.

See how many of the small pictures you can match up to the big pictures

cooking

floor

light

heating

ceiling

lavatory

window

door

wall

bed

LONG AGO

See how many of the small pictures you can match up to the big pictures

light

window

floor

lavatory

ceiling

bed

heating

wall

cooking

door

VERY LONG AGO

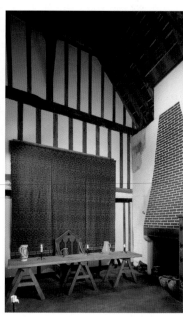

See how many of the small pictures you can match up to the big pictures

light

lavatory

door

heating

cooking

floor

wall

bed

window

ceiling

FAMOUS PEOPLE AND EVENTS

STORIES AS TIMELINES

Stories are generally more memorable if they are accompanied by pictures. You can go one better than this and make a connection between imagination and reality by introducing your class to three-dimensional material from the time of the story. The simplest way to do this is to capitalise on what your town has to offer by way of buildings or objects in your local museum. If your town is fairly old, pick out buildings or places associated with one particular period, and work out a route that takes in some of them. Choose someone famous from that time and use the events

in that person's life, or notable inventions or discoveries that happened during that time, to make up a timeline in class. Then take your class on your trail around town, making drawings or taking photographs of features from the same period to add into the timeline back in class.

MAKING A TIMELINE

Introduce the idea of timelines to your class by starting with a timeline of a child of their age. Cut out pictures of a very small baby in a crib, a child in a pushchair, on a tricycle or toy car, on a bike, and lastly a child in school. Give a pic-

ture each to five pupils, and let the rest of the class, working together, move the holders of the pictures about in a line until they have arranged them into chronological order. Stretch a washing line on the floor in front of the human timeline, and attach the first picture to it. Ask someone to measure out one foot's length from the first picture and add the second picture there, and so on. Explain that each foot's span represents a year, then calculate the age of the historical figure whose timeline you want to do, and ask one pupil to measure it out in foot spans along a new line.

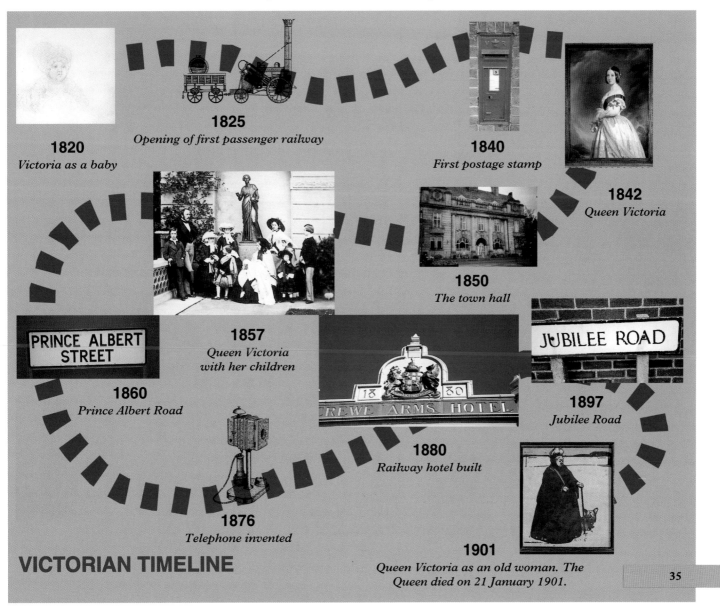

1820
Victoria as a baby

1825
Opening of first passenger railway

1840
First postage stamp

1842
Queen Victoria

1850
The town hall

PRINCE ALBERT STREET

1857
Queen Victoria with her children

JUBILEE ROAD

1860
Prince Albert Road

1897
Jubilee Road

1880
Railway hotel built

1876
Telephone invented

1901
Queen Victoria as an old woman. The Queen died on 21 January 1901.

VICTORIAN TIMELINE

BIG PICTURE BOOK

If you are within travelling distance of a place where a famous event happened, use it to help your pupils create their own story using a simple storyboard. Tell your own version of the event first, show any pictures you have, and then ask the class for words which describe the main character. Why not make use of the Literacy Hour for this? Pupils can draw the main person in their storyboard, adding the name, and anything they can write about what he or she was like.

On site, encourage pupils to relate as much of the story as they can remember, and find out where the events happened. Ask for words to describe the place, and how pupils think the character felt, and get a helper to note them down. They can draw the different events of the story, using the background they can see, but adding their own figures.

Back in school, group your pupils into sets of five and let them transfer one illustration each from their storyboard, including one made into a cover picture, onto large sheets of sugar paper. Use the pictures to remind pupils of the words they collected, and discuss simple sentences that they can write under the pictures (or word process and paste on) to form the story. Bind these together to produce big picture books, and swap them around so that groups can read each other's work to the rest of the class.

Charles I with his family.

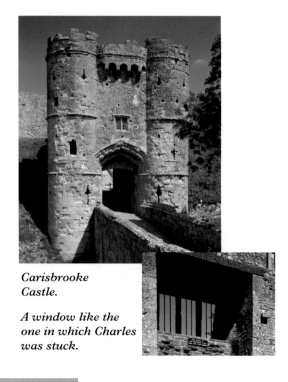

Carisbrooke Castle.

A window like the one in which Charles was stuck.

> *King Charles was captured by Parliament's army and was imprisoned in Carisbrooke Castle on the Isle of Wight. He tried to escape through a window but got stuck between the bars. He was caught and returned to prison.*

A STORYBOARD

MAKE A DRAMA

Instead of writing and drawing the event, your class could make their own play based on it. You may actually live near to the scene of a famous event, like a battle, or where someone showed exceptional courage or where something was launched or used for the first time. If not, find out what historic places there are locally that would provide somewhere safe for you to work with your class, and choose an event from that period. Tell the story during Literacy Hour, and again on site, with the class filling in the exciting bits.

Discuss with them how the characters might feel and react, and if the place that they are in might have an effect on this. For instance, is it a cold, windy place which would make the historical characters shiver and hunch themselves up, or is it a huge, intimidating room, which might make them feel small and nervous?

Talk together about how emotions can be expressed not just in the face but also by body language, by getting them to freeze into different appropriate poses. You may need to start with situations that

they already know about first, like finding a spider in the bath. Work the 'freezes' up into groups forming tableaux of the story, and then talk together about what each character might say, or think, at that point.

You can either finish your drama here, as a series of tableaux with each pupil contributing a line or even just a word, and you providing the linking storyline between each group, or use the tableaux as an end or starting point to a scene, with pupils acting out the story.

Boscobel House, Shropshire.

The open trap door to the priest's hole is under the window.

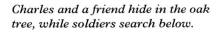

Charles and a friend hide in the oak tree, while soldiers search below.

Mʳ Iane Lane and King:

Charles escapes with Lady Jane Lane.

Prince Charles, son of Charles I, escaped to Boscobel House after being defeated in battle. Firstly he hid in an oak tree all day whilst the army searched in the bushes underneath, and the next day he crouched in a priest hole, about one metre square, just beneath the floorboards at the top of the house. Charles was nearly two metres tall. He escaped by dressing up as the servant of Lady Jane Lane, who lived nearby, and they fled to France. Charles later returned and became King Charles II.

THE ROMANS IN BRITAIN

WHO WERE THE ROMANS?

The Romans were a whole mix of different peoples - 60 million people living in a number of different provinces which made up the Roman Empire. Although it is difficult to say exactly when Rome began to develop, the Romans used to teach their children that the city was founded in 753 BC. It was over a thousand years later that the Roman Empire came to an end.

ROMAN BRITAIN

But how did Britain fit into this huge empire? The province of Britannia was added in the first century AD and was on the furthest limits of the Roman world. While it is clearly important to us, as a significant part of our early history, it was only a very small, and mostly insignificant, part of the Roman Empire.

It is important to help pupils understand that the Romans did not come to an empty barren landscape, inhabited only by a few uncivilised tribes but that the native Britons already had complex societies and sophisticated cultures.

Conquest

The Romans invaded Britain on three separate occasions. Julius Caesar led expeditions in 55 and 54 BC and, after winning some battles, made treaty arrangements with and imposed taxes on some of the tribes.

The conquest of Britain did not begin until AD 43 when an army of 40,000, sent by the Emperor Claudius, landed at Richborough and defeated the tribes of the south east and established Britain as a province of the Roman Empire, with a permanent Roman presence.

A province of Rome

The first Roman sites were built for and by the army. Civilian settlements (called *vici*) grew up around the forts. As the army moved on to conquer more of the island, some of these sites became towns, often populated by retired soldiers. By about AD 60 most of England south and east of a line from the Wash to the Bristol Channel was under Roman control.

By the second century a very large part of Britain was Roman. Its limits to the north were defined by Hadrian's Wall (Hadrian visited Britain in AD 122) and later by the Antonine Wall.

In the end Britain was a prosperous province for some time but by the late third century was beginning to suffer attacks along its southern shores from Saxons and Gauls. In the fourth century the power of the Roman Empire was waning and Britain was ruled by usurpers who had seized power.

In the early years of the fifth century more troops were removed and from about AD 407 the Roman administration probably ceased to pay the few troops left in Britain. In AD 410 the Emperor Honorius wrote to the British that they could no longer rely on the Roman Empire for support and that they must look to their own defences.

Building Hadrian's Wall.

Building Hadrian's Wall

The stone and earth frontier of Hadrian's Wall stretched 117 kilometres across northern Britain. At the time of the conquest of Britain, soldiers did not normally serve in the province where they had been

Hadrian's Wall.

born. The Wall was built and manned by soldiers from a number of the provinces in the north-western parts of the empire, from Hungary and Bulgaria, for example, as well as those from Gaul and Germany.

LIFE IN ROMAN BRITAIN

The occupation of Britain by the Romans brought a number of new aspects to life for people in the province. Each of these topics provides opportunities for extension work in other curriculum subjects.

Leisure

People all over the Roman world went in very large numbers to see performances of various sorts:

■ to attend plays, concerts and poetry readings in a theatre

■ to see shows of gladiatorial combat, often involving fights with wild animals in an amphitheatre

■ to watch, and bet on, chariot racing in a stadium.

Civic pride

Roman citizens expected to find the same sorts of buildings, and facilities, all over the Empire. The town council needed to develop

■ buildings for town administration and business - a *forum* (a large

An artist's impression of the market place at Letocetum (Wall in Staffordshire) in the second century AD.

open space) for business, open air meetings and ceremonies, perhaps a *macellum* (a market hall), a *basilica* (a very large aisled hall) for town administration, law courts or business

■ places for entertainment and leisure - public baths, perhaps a theatre or amphitheatre

■ a range of temples

■ basic services, such as streets, rubbish collection, water supply and sewage facilities.

Industry

Some industries, such as the mining of metal ores, came under government control but many others were carried out by individual craftsmen working inside towns, such as potters and leather workers.

Religion

For the Romans, religion was part of everyday life. Every house had a small shrine where the statues of the *lares*, the gods of the household, were kept. In towns you would expect to find temples, statues and altars to a number of different gods, for example:

■ the main Roman gods and goddesses, Jupiter, Juno and Minerva

■ lesser gods but connected with a particular aspect of life such as trade

■ the Emperor

■ native gods and Roman gods combined, such as Sulis (Celtic) Minerva (Roman) and in later periods Christian churches.

Burial

It was forbidden, under Roman law, to bury anyone within the limits or walls of a town. Roads leading out of settlements were usually lined with tombs and simpler burial places. You will find evidence from Roman burials in tombstones in museums.

Reconstruction drawing of Silchester Roman town.

A ROMAN VILLA

LULLINGSTONE ROMAN VILLA

Lullingstone Roman Villa lay at the heart of a large agricultural estate. Dating from the first century AD, it was occupied for nearly 250 years. In the second century the villa was remodelled and a bath suite added. At the end of the third century an underfloor heating system was installed in three rooms and intricate mosaics laid. Towards the end of the fourth century the villa building was altered to accommodate a Christian chapel.

AD 100-150
Evidence

Small villa building constructed of timber and clay on footings of mortared flint (locally available stone). A block of rooms had a verandah in front and two projecting wings, one of which had a cellar below.

Interpretation

The quality of the building's construction suggests that the owner was a Romano-British farmer. The plan of the villa is typical of many built in this period of prosperity in Roman Britain. The cellar may have been used for storing food.

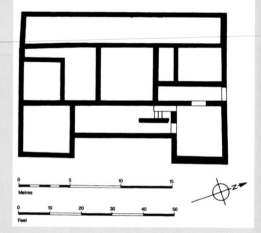

Plan of the first masonry villa.

AD 150-275
Evidence

The villa is extensively altered. The basic plan was added to on each end. The cellar now has other stairs built and has elaborate wall paintings. In the second phase of alterations a bath-suite is added to the southern end of the villa. Finds from the excavations of this period include fine quality pottery and glass.

Interpretation

The wealth shown in both the finds and the alterations to the house suggest a very rich owner. The baths alone indicate great expense, not only in the construction but also in the slaves/servants needed to maintain and run it.

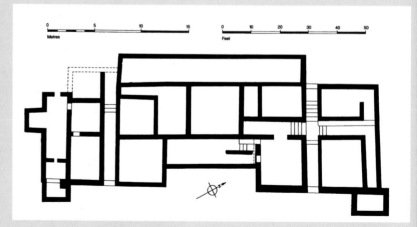

Plan of the remodelled villa, with the baths added, AD 150-200.

AD 275-350
Evidence

At the end of the third century the villa is remodelled again with a row of heated rooms added. The baths were converted and enlarged. In the mid-fourth century a large dining room was added in a style found in other villas and town houses throughout the Empire. Mosaic floors are also laid including one with a Latin text. Carved busts from this period were found stored in the cellar after AD 350. A large granary and a temple-mausoleum were built at this time outside the main villa building.

Interpretation

The owners were clearly wealthy to rebuild and decorate the villa but the busts, which were carved in the Mediterranean style, indicate an important person coming to the province of Britain from a more central part of the Roman Empire.

The size of the granary suggests that the villa was the centre of a large agricultural estate.

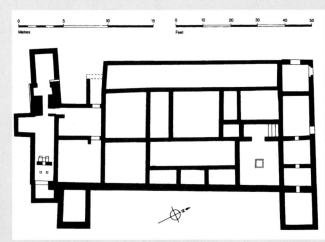

Plan of the villa, about AD 275-350, with a row of heated rooms at the north end.

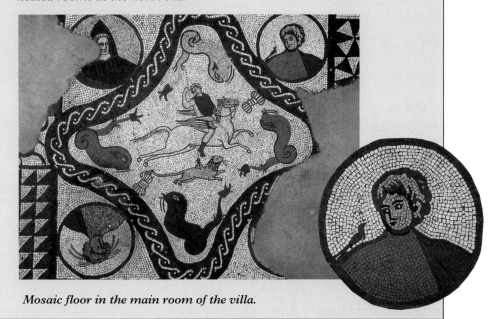

Mosaic floor in the main room of the villa.

AD 350-425
Evidence

The heated rooms and rooms over the cellar on the north side of the villa are converted into a chapel and ante room. Wall paintings with Christian symbols and figures decorated the walls. There was evidence of occupation into the fifth century but the baths were in disuse. A serious fire gutted much of the house.

Interpretation

The family had adopted Christianity and were still using the house. Perhaps in the early fifth century the villa became unoccupied but we think the chapel remained in use.

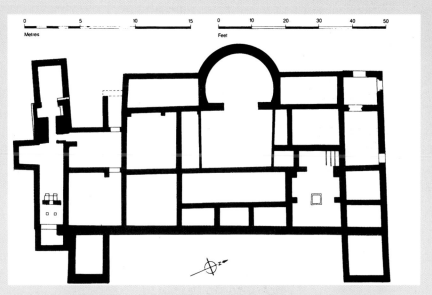

Plan of the villa after AD 350-425, showing the large apsed dining room.

THE ANGLO-SAXONS

WHO WERE THE ANGLO-SAXONS?

Before the end of the fourth century AD, the coasts around Britain were under attack from a number of new invaders. The Irish and the Picts attacked the west and the north. Saxons and other peoples, together known as Anglo-Saxons, sailed across from Europe.

Anglo-Saxon is the name we use now to describe several different peoples:

■ Angles, Saxons and Jutes came from northern Germany and Scandinavia

■ Frisians and Franks came from lands which are now part of France, Holland and part of Germany.

An artist's impression of the Anglo-Saxon village of West Heslerton in North Yorkshire which has been excavated. Archaeologists found houses and workshops dating from about AD 450 to 650.

DUMNONIA Celtic and British kingdoms
ESSEX Anglo-Saxon kingdoms
------ Offas Dyke

The Anglo-Saxons gradually pushed the Britons westwards:

conquests by 600

conquests by 800

0   100   200 km

SETTLING IN BRITAIN

By the middle of the fifth century there were Anglo-Saxons settled in the eastern part of Britain, from north of the Humber to the south coast. Gradually the Anglo-Saxons moved west, driving out the British warlords and, by the beginning of the sixth century, they had settled widely in Britain.

Villages and cemeteries

Archaeologists have discovered and excavated a number of Anglo-Saxon settlements (see page 44) and burial sites. Anglo-Saxons were often buried with objects which they might need for their journey to the afterlife such as clothes, jewellery and other valuable possessions. Swords and spears are often found buried with men but everyday objects are also common - combs made of bone, knives and brooches, for example.

Anglo-Saxon clothes

Evidence from burial sites allows us to tell what some Anglo-Saxons wore. Women often wore long flowing gowns fastened at the shoulder with big brooches, and at the waist they had a purse hanging from a belt. They wore jewellery of all sorts including necklaces, pins, rings and bracelets. Men usually wore short tunics, leggings and laced boots. They also wore cloaks fastened with big brooches.

Sutton Hoo

One of the most remarkable discoveries from this period was the grave of an Anglo-Saxon leader at Sutton Hoo in Suffolk. The leader, who may have been Raewald, a king of East Anglia who died in about AD 625, was buried in a ship with a remarkable collection of fine objects (now to be seen in the British Museum).

THE COMING OF CHRISTIANITY

Christianity had been introduced into Ireland in the fifth century and an Irish monk, Columba, founded a monastery on the island of Iona on the west coast of Scotland. Missionaries came from there to settle on the island of Lindisfarne in the kingdom of Northumbria (see page 26). In AD 597 Pope Gregory I sent a group of about fifty missionaries, led by Augustine, to convert the English. King Aethelbert of Kent received the missionaries and allowed them to build a church in Canterbury. Augustine became England's first archbishop.

Monasteries and learning

Between AD 650 and 850 Anglo-Saxon kings and their bishops built hundreds of monasteries. These early monasteries included a variety of people as well as priests, nuns and monks. The monasteries, with churches which were often elaborately built in stone, became centres of learning and art. Some monks, skilled in calligraphy and drawing, copied the stories of the Bible and the lives of saints for others to read. These manuscripts were often beautifully decorated.

In the monastery at Jarrow in Northumbria, the greatest Anglo-Saxon scholar, Bede, wrote his *Ecclesiastical History of the English People*, finished in AD 731.

PROTECTING THE KINGDOMS

By the time of Bede Anglo-Saxon kings were becoming more powerful and ruled over larger areas of the country. In the seventh and eighth centuries the kingdom of Mercia was the richest and strongest. The Mercian king, Offa, who ruled from AD 738 to 796, controlled more resources than any other king and was regarded by some as the king of all England.

In the 780s Offa decided to put a stop to the Welsh tribes who kept raiding his western borders. He built a great ditch up to 2.5 metres high and up to 20 metres wide to keep them out. His great dyke can still be seen.

But Anglo-Saxon power was not to last. Towards the end of the eighth century everything was to change again as new invaders appeared (see page 46).

Excavations at Sutton Hoo in 1939 revealed only the impression of the ship's timbers. The helmet was only one of a number of finely-made metal objects. It is made of iron with overlays of bronze, silver and gold picturing scenes of fighting.

CASE STUDY AN ANGLO-SAXON VILLAGE

A large number of Anglo-Saxon settlements have been identified from land surveys, aerial photography and from excavation. There were different types of settlement, from farmsteads for a single family to villages. Some villages are quite small (perhaps up to eight houses) but others are more extensive. The settlement at Mucking in Essex was found to have over two hundred buildings when excavated.

WEST STOW

The Anglo-Saxon village of West Stow in Suffolk has been almost completely excavated and partly reconstructed. The site was excavated between 1965 and 1972 and is now open to the public. An Anglo-Saxon cemetery had been discovered there in the nineteenth century. The village itself survived because it was protected by a sand dune which had blown over it in a great storm around 1300.

Anglo-Saxon settlers chose West Stow to live in around AD 420. By about AD 600 the villagers began to drift away and by AD 650 West Stow was completely abandoned.

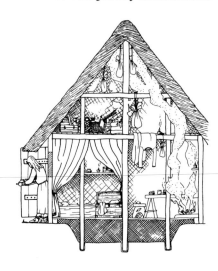

Sunken floor building.

The village and its buildings

Only three or four families lived in the small village of West Stow - called Stowa in the Domesday Book. Each family had two sorts of buildings, both made of wood with thatched roofs. One (called a hall by archaeologists) had a hearth in the centre. The other type of building is called a sunken house. It had a wooden tent-like structure over a dug-out area below the wooden floor. Sometimes people lived in these sunken houses, but usually they were workshops or stores.

Skilled craftspeople came to the village regularly to make pottery, pins and combs from bone and objects of iron, such as knives.

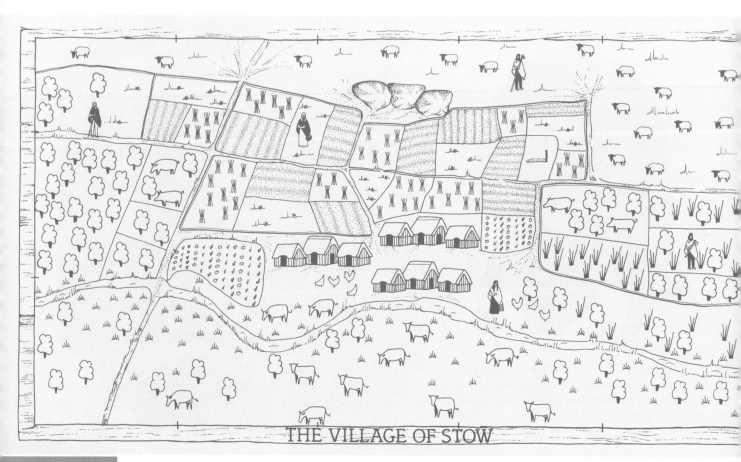

THE VILLAGE OF STOW

West Stow 'hall' building.

Reconstructed building at West Stow.

The river was a source of water, fish and birds and was also a means of communication.

Food and farming

The people of Stowa farmed the land around them. Archaeological evidence tells us that they cultivated wheat, rye, barley, oats and peas in the fields around the village. We know that they bred animals because the bones of cattle, sheep, pigs, geese and chickens have been found. We also know that they hunted (deer and wild fowl) and fished to add to their diet. They also kept horses, dogs and cats.

USING WEST STOW

The village is open for visiting schools (details on page 71) and has a visitor centre as well as a good range of resource material for teachers and pupils. Several buildings have been reconstructed with some furniture and fittings and sometimes there are costumed interpreters on site.

THE VIKINGS

WHO WERE THE VIKINGS?

The Vikings came from Scandinavia, countries now known as Norway, Sweden and Denmark. The name 'Viking' comes from the word *vikingr* which means pirate or raider. Vikings were not always raiders, some were also traders and travelled throughout Europe selling goods and slaves. They first attacked Britain in AD 793 at Lindisfarne and continued to raid and attack until they controlled large areas of north and east England.

Why they came to Britain

They first came to plunder - seeking treasure and slaves, attacking all down the east coast of England. They knew of the wealth donated by kings to monasteries.

As the Scandinavian population increased the division of land could not support large families. Many Norwegian Viking farmsteads clung to the sides of mountains or the sides of fjords where there was not much arable land to divide up. Britain and North Europe, however, had a much warmer climate than the homelands of the Vikings and the land was often much easier to farm. When they settled they became farmers and fishermen.

This gravestone from Lindisfarne is believed to show Vikings attacking the island with their swords and axes poised for attack.

How did they get here?

The Vikings sailed to other lands in longboats. These were cleverly designed and could sail fast under sail power or manpower. They were ideal for exploration and as a weapon of conquest. The hull was shallow for river travel and shaped to run ashore at speed on beaches. It was light enough to be carried overland to the next river or rolled along on logs. The ships could be up to 25 metres long and 6 metres wide. Around 36 men could man the oars. The sails were 10 metres broad and 6 metres high. The prow was carved into a monstrous figure of a dragon to strike terror into an enemy.

VIKING WARRIORS

An Arab traveller who came across Viking warriors in Russia wrote: 'They have huge bodies and great courage. Each warrior usually carries with him some craftsman's tools such as an axe. He fights on foot with a spear and a shield. He

Artist's impression of the quayside at Viking Jorvik (York).

carries a sword and dagger and has athrowing spear slung across his back.'

The warriors fighting in Russia probably wore tunics of padded leather with heavy chain-mail shirts over the top. On their heads they wore helmets with protective strips which covered their noses and surrounded their eyes. These helmets did not have horns. Chain-mail protected their necks.

Weapons

Their weapons included spears, axes with a blade needing two hands, and brightly coloured wooden circular shields.

Swords were highly prized, with names like 'Leg-biter' and 'Gleam of Battle'.

VIKING LIFE

Not all Viking men were warriors. Most were farmers, growing crops such as wheat, barley and rye and keeping animals such as sheep, goats, cattle, pigs, and chickens. Others hunted or fished using hooks, nets and harpoons to catch fish, seals, walruses and whales. The women worked in the home, preparing meals, looking after children, making clothes and looking

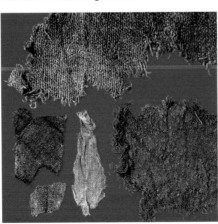

The ends of leather straps were often finished with a decorative end. This tiny one (6.2 cm long), found in Viking York, has been carved with plant decoration.

after the animals.

They lived as large extended families usually in one house. The main room was used for sleeping and eating and was heated by an open fireplace or hearth in the middle with only a hole in the roof to let out the smoke. Windows did not have glass; wooden shutters were used instead. They slept on raised platforms and wrapped themselves in rugs and animal furs to keep warm.

Viking clothes

Most of their clothes were made from wool or linen. Rich people could afford more expensive materials such as silk. They liked to wear colourful clothes and both men and women wore jewellery. Viking men and women liked to look good, and some ironed their clothes using heavy lumps of glass heated on a fire. We know that they also combed their hair, beards and moustaches as beautifully carved combs have been found made from deer's antler or bone.

Men hung their personal belongings such as a knife, comb or purse from their belt. From a brooch women hung personal objects

Shallow wooden platter.

A variety of Viking woollen textiles found on excavations in York.

such as a knife, comb, and keys (valuables were stored in chests with strong locks).

Women wore long dresses and shawls which were often patterned. They wore their hair long and knotted. Those who could afford jewellery wore brooches, huge arm-rings and glass beads.

Men wore a shirt, trousers and long tunic. Their cloaks were fastened at the right shoulder or hip (so keeping the sword arm free) by a brooch or ring pin. On their feet they wore shoes made of leather.

VIKING AFTERLIFE

Viking warriors believed death in combat was the greatest honour you could achieve. Once dead they were immediately taken to Asgard, the home of the gods. Odin's handmaidens, the Valkyries, would take them to his hall, Valhalla, where they would be served drink as their wounds healed.

Wealthy warriors were often buried or cremated with all the goods that they would need for the life hereafter - food and drink, clothes, sword, horse, dog and ship (to carry them to the next world). Longboats were used for the burials of Viking kings and queens and legends say that some Viking warlords were cremated in their longships as they sailed into the night.

VIKING GODS

The Vikings believed in many gods. Some of our weekdays are named after Viking gods.

Tuesday is named after Tyr, god of warriors.

Wednesday is named after Woden (Germanic spelling) or Odin

Thursday is named after Thor, god of thunder

Friday is named after Freya, the goddess of fertility

A VIKING TOWN

The bustling modern city of York, now a place which attracts thousands of tourists, has a very long history revealed by archaeologists in recent excavations throughout the city. It was once a legionary fortress and was then one of the main towns of Roman Britain. Roman records tell us it was called Eburacum. Later it became the Anglo-Saxon capital of Northumbria and was called Eoforwic.

THE COMING OF THE VIKINGS

In AD 865 a 'great army' (as the English called it) of Vikings landed in East Anglia to begin an extended campaign in England. They headed straight for Eoforwic and attacked the town on 1 November 866. They captured the city easily as the Northumbrians were divided by civil war. The Vikings left an Anglo-Saxon called Egbert to rule in their name.

Although the Northumbrians regrouped in an attempt to drive out the Vikings in 867, they were unsuccessful and a great number were killed. In 876 part of the 'great army', under the leadership of Halfdan, settled in and around the town which they now called Jorvik and made it the capital of the kingdom of York. Jorvik remained the centre of the Viking kingdom until 954.

A trading centre

When the Vikings first came to York it was already a busy trading centre. It stands on the River Ouse and ships could easily reach it from the North Sea. Viking Jorvik was a large bustling place of about 10,000 people, described by one writer who visited it as 'filled with treasures of merchants from many lands'. But Jorvik was also known for its crafts and industries. Many

After excavations in York's city centre, some Viking remains were preserved and a reconstruction built for visitors.

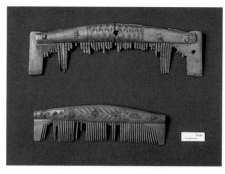

Combs made from antler, found at Coppergate.

different goods were made there including glass beads, combs, hairpins, needles and gaming counters of bone and a large variety of leather objects, such as shoes and purses.

Viking houses

Archaeologists have found a number of Viking houses in a street called Coppergate. The word *gata* is a Danish Viking word for 'street'. The word 'copper' comes from the cupmakers (*koppr* means cup) who had their workshops there. The remains of the houses show us how ordinary people lived. The houses

were quite small (about 7 by 4.4 metres) built inside long strips of land running back from the street and divided from neighbouring plots by wooden wattle fences. The houses were also built of wood and were open inside with no inner walls. The family slept and ate in the one space with an open fire in the centre. There may have been benches against the walls and perhaps a table and a chest to store valuables, bedding and clothes. The area at the back of houses was filled with workshops, yards, storage and rubbish pits and cesspits.

The remains of a side wall of a Viking house at Coppergate showing the construction of planks and posts.

THE JORVIK VIKING CENTRE

After the excavations at Coppergate were finished a project was developed to preserve some of the remains *in situ*. The Jorvik Viking Centre now welcomes visitors to investigate the real remains of the houses and the thousands of objects which came from them as well as careful reconstructions and what archaeologists think the evidence tells us. The Jorvik Viking Centre is therefore a good place for schools to

■ see real evidence from the Viking period

■ find out about the archaeological process from excavation to conservation of objects

■ observe and ask questions about the reconstructions.

Information on page 71 includes details about the Centre and also about the nearby Archaeological Resource Centre (ARC).

Model of the an archaeological laboratory at the Centre showing material from Coppergate being studied and conserved.

Visitors travel in 'Time Cars' (with a spoken commentary) through a reconstructed street alongside the quay in the Jorvik Viking Centre.

VIKING NAMES

The names of many of our towns and villages can be attributed to the Vikings. This is as a result of land distribution which saw large areas broken up into smaller units which would need new names. Endings to place names often have Viking origins:

by - village
beck - stream
biggin(g) - building
borough - fort
car(r) - brushwood, especially on swampy ground
dale - valley
fell - hill
force - waterfall
forth - fjord
garth - enclosure or garden
gate - track/path
gill - deep glen with stream at bottom
haven - harbours
hesket/hesketh - horse-race or horse track
holm - small island in river or bay
ing - pasture/meadow
keld - well or spring
kirk - church
lund - grove
mire - bog or swamp
nes - headland
raise - cairn
scale - house
scar/skear - isolated rock in the sea
scough/scow - wood
slack - slope on edge of mountain
tarn - pond
thorp - a smaller settlement or outpost of an estate
thwaite - clearing
toft - piece of ground
wath - ford
wick - market places
with - wood

A reconstruction of a Viking house at the Jorvik Viking Centre.

TUDOR LIFE

THE TUDOR PERIOD

The Tudor period began when Henry Tudor was crowned Henry VII after defeating Richard III in a war which practically annihilated the aristocracy. Following a period of peace and consolidation, his son, Henry VIII, stirred up radical changes when he broke with Rome, closed the monasteries and provoked invasion from France.

The pot of religious unrest simmered quietly throughout the short reign of Edward VI, and boiled over under Catholic Mary. Only under the last Tudor monarch, Elizabeth I, who died in 1603, was a sense of tolerance and continuity restored.

Many buildings from the period are left to show the changes that happened. The ruins of the once powerful abbeys remain, as do the massive fortifications along the south coast. The new breed of opportunistic courtiers, who replaced the aristocracy, built themselves great houses (some in the remains of monasteries) to show off their new status, and some went further and founded colleges, schools and other public buildings. Not so grand, but more likely to be in travelling distance of your school, are the town houses of the merchants, or the brick or timber-framed halls of the small landowners.

CLUES TO LOOK FOR IN TUDOR BUILDINGS

When King Henry VIII closed the monasteries, he also displaced the leaders of architectural fashion. Up until then the grand palaces had tended to copy the gothic doorways and traceried windows of the abbeys. With a temporary halt put on ecclesiastical building, the classical influence, which had been slowly creeping in, began to gain

more ground.

Major elements, like symmetry, and the rectangular shape of windows, were adopted, and decorative details, like classical columns, pediments and friezes began to appear on grand buildings. But people still favoured elements from the previous age, like the towers, turrets and battlements which had been an essential feature of castles, and which now became busy additions to private and public buildings. When the popularity of these started to fade they were replaced by the Elizabethan love of devices like initials and scrolls.

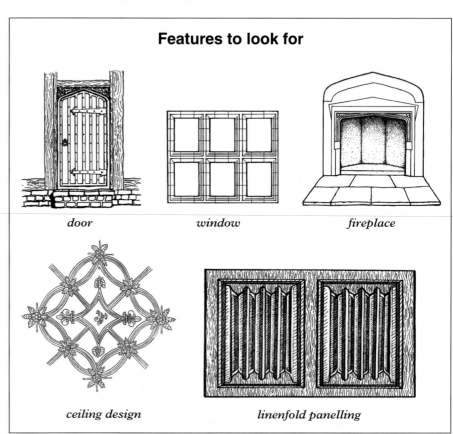

Features to look for

door *window* *fireplace*

ceiling design *linenfold panelling*

Titchfield Abbey, Hampshire, was converted into a Tudor mansion. The gatehouse, with its battlements and towers, looks back to the medieval period, but the clean straight lines of the windows and the balanced towers make the building look symmetrical.

Building materials

Advances in technology had a huge influence on how buildings looked. Developments in the manufacture of glass made it more available and at less cost, so windows became larger. The panes of glass were still small, held together with lead strips often in decorative patterns.

Brick became the new prestigious building material. It was easier to handle than stone, uniform in size and as it was more resistant to heat, it enabled people to have as many fireplaces as they could afford, and led to a proliferation of chimney stacks. Up until now, most ordinary homes had a central hearth from which smoke escaped through the roof, and were therefore usually single storied, or the hearth was in a hall which rose the whole height of the house. Now more storeys could be added, and the old high-ceilinged hall had a dividing floor inserted.

Fireplaces were a tremendous advance in terms of comfort, and it also encouraged decoration of ceilings where before the sooty deposits left by smoke made this impracticable.

New techniques in carpentry gave rise to fashionable, highly ornate staircases, and widespread use of wainscotting, or wooden panels, to line interior walls, making rooms warmer. Many of these were carved to represent folds of linen.

BUILDINGS FOR DEFENCE

As protection against the threat of attack from France, Henry VIII built a string of forts along the south coast.

The forts accommodated a huge number of cannon, but they also had to withstand fire as well as deliver it. For this they needed very thick walls, and a rounded shape to deflect and reduce the

The gatehouse of Stokesay Castle in Shropshire has a timber-framed structure with carved ornamentation.

Deal Castle in Kent has a central, drum-like living area with cannons on it, surrounded by two lower levels of semi-circular gun platforms.

impact of the cannon balls. Unlike medieval castles, these forts were not baronial homes, but were garrisons for trained men, and accommodation was basic.

TIMBER-FRAMED HOUSES

In areas where stone, or clay for brick-making, were not plentiful, people lived in timber-framed houses. The wooden parts were made to fit before they were put up, rather like a kit. Carpenters' marks, identifying the pieces, are often still visible.

As trees became scarcer, shorter straight sections of wood were used, and the pattern of close uprights gave way to more widely-spaced timbers strengthened by cross braces. Later still, even smaller sections were used, giving rise to intricate patterns. The infill was often wattle and daub, which consisted of interwoven branches plastered over with mud, reinforced by dung or chopped straw. As bricks became cheaper they were used in a herringbone pattern as the infill.

To give extra space and stability, the upper storeys could be built slightly larger than the one beneath, creating an overhang called a jetty. In towns this led to street houses leaning out towards each other, blocking out light and increasing the fire hazard.

CASE STUDY

THE TUDOR HOUSE

Throughout the medieval period and into Tudor times, the dwellings of the rich were home to large households, including not only the owner's family, but also high-ranking servants, semi-permanent guests and extended family, and a vast range of servants. Housing all these at the beginning of the medieval period had been simple; everyone lived, ate, slept, and carried out business in a great hall, except for the lord's family and guests, who used a private room at one end, and cooking, which went on in rooms or buildings at the other end.

KIRBY HALL

Kirby Hall in Northamptonshire was completed in about 1590 by Sir Christopher Hatton, a favourite courtier of Elizabeth I. It is now roofless in parts. It was designed to make a grand statement about its owner, and from a distance gives an impression of symmetry and order, with matching windows, chimneys and gables. Guests entered via a long avenue of trees into an outer courtyard, and then an inner courtyard before entering the interior. The prolonged access was a deliberate ploy to ensure visitors were aware of the magnificence of the building and therefore the wealth and power of the owner.

Inside, another long walk awaited guests. After waiting in the Great Hall, a massive room used for entertaining, while a servant informed the lord, they would ascend the great staircase and pass through the State Rooms, a series of progressively higher status rooms, until, if they were important enough, they reached the lord's Best Bedchamber. This was a public, not a private room like bedrooms now. The State Rooms included the Great Chamber, where family meals were served,

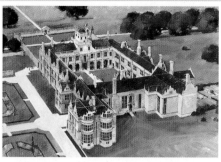

Artist's impression of Kirby Hall.

Kirby Hall, Northamptonshire.

the Great Withdrawing Room, which may have contained, among other things, a billiards table, and the Best Bedroom. Smaller rooms, called pallet chambers, lay between some of the bedrooms; this was where personal servants slept on a removeable pallet or mattress.

Another important room was the Long Gallery, which has now disappeared, and which was where exercise was taken on rainy days, and where the family portraits

The South Range at Kirby, showing the huge symmetrical windows, pilasters, frieze and the highly decorated porch. The bust and balcony are later additions.

were hung. It spread along the whole of the upper floor of one range of the courtyard; the rest of the ranges were high-ranking servants' and guests' quarters. There are no bathrooms at Kirby - water was carried to hip baths in bedrooms, and the equivalent of the lavatory was a close stool, which contained a pot to be emptied by a servant.

The kitchens were well away from the State Rooms, in their traditional position at the other side of the Great Hall. This was to ensure that no smells or sounds of cooking permeated there, but it did mean that servants had a long way to carry food.

The fashionable house

The man employed to build Kirby was Thomas Thorpe, who used fashionable classical details from the new books on architectural design which were coming over from the continent. The inner courtyard shows many of these copied designs; a loggia, columns, friezes, scallop shells, vases and carvings. Huge windows occupy either side of the entrance porch to the house. At this point the old fights with the new - the window on the right is large because it is part of the impressive two-storey hall, and important rooms always had large windows. The window to the left of the porch matches it to display the new trend for classical symmetry, but the rooms behind it belong to the service area, which would not normally have large windows. The space behind is actually divided horizontally to accommodate the first floor rooms.

The Elizabethans lived in an age of exploration of new lands, in which voyagers brought back exotic plants and fruit. This fed a Tudor desire for impressive gardens, full of new plants. Kirby's garden is symmetrically arranged, and was regarded as a place for formal recreation - an extension of the living space. In order to create it, the village church and graveyard were removed.

VISITING HOUSES

If you intend to visit a furnished house, ask pupils to write a list of the rooms they would find in a modern house. On site, they can use this as a checklist, adding to it all the extra rooms which have no modern equivalent, like the Great Hall, which will give you the opportunity to open up the discussion about difference in lifestyle between now and then. The checklist will also lead to questions about rooms which they might expect to find, but which are missing in a Tudor house, like the bathroom. Preparation for visiting an unfurnished or partly ruined house is different, as the indications to the function of the room have to be looked for more carefully. Clues to look for are:

■ size - the larger and taller the room the more important it generally was

■ windows - high status rooms had the largest windows

■ doors - impressive rooms often had impressive doorways

■ fireplaces - the presence of a fireplace indicated a living room, rather than one used for storage. Size and decoration reflected the room's status, except for the kitchen, where the fireplace was huge but plain

■ wall, floor and ceiling covering - the quality of these reflects the importance and sometimes the function of the room. Channels in the floor leading to drains shows a kitchen or storage area

■ position - where a room is in relation to other rooms may tell you about its function. For example, an undecorated, windowless room near a kitchen is likely to be a storage or service area.

Pupils can enter what they think the function of the rooms were onto a blank plan, and then compare their deductions with the official plan. A good exercise in encouraging pupils to think hard about what the house was like when lived in is to ask them to create their own interpretation panels for the site, telling others, perhaps younger pupils, how the rooms were used and furnished. This can be a stimulus for their own research back in school and could lead to their own drawings, based on sketches they make during the visit, on how each room may have originally looked.

The Great Hall as it is now, and (right) as it may have looked in the Tudor period.

An artist's impression of the Best Bedchamber.

VICTORIA'S ENGLAND

Queen Victoria reigned from 1837 till 1901. Her long reign saw candle lighting give way to gas then to electricity, the introduction of state education, transport revolutionised by the spread of the railways, and Charles Darwin's ideas on evolution challenging the basis of society. Throughout all these changes the figure of Victoria remained constant, as the head of the country and its empire.

WHO WAS QUEEN VICTORIA?

Victoria was born in London, in 1819. Her father, the Duke of Kent, died when she was only eight months old and her uncle, King William IV, had no children, so Victoria became the heir to the throne. From the age of thirteen she kept a diary, writing it daily until she died, filling 122 volumes with details of her thoughts and activities.

In 1840, the young Queen married her cousin, Prince Albert of Saxe-Coburg. In November the same year their first child, Victoria, was born; she was followed by eight more brothers and sisters.

OSBORNE HOUSE

The family had three royal residences: Buckingham Palace, Windsor Castle and the Royal Pavilion at Brighton, but none of these was suitable for the private needs of a young, growing family. Victoria longed for a place where she could relax, away from the public eye, and Albert wanted to replicate some of the experiences of his own childhood for his children.

The Queen knew and liked the Isle of Wight, having visited it twice as a child. Osborne House was chosen as the family's holiday home. It was close enough to London, yet its island location ensured its seclusion. However, the house was too small for the royal family and the household. Thomas Cubitt was employed to build a new wing, and then to demolish the existing house and to build further wings for the royal household and guests. The entire cost was to be met from the private income of Victoria and Albert. The family moved in after the first phase of building was completed in 1846.

The children had a 'Swiss Cottage' in the grounds, where they played and learned about housekeeping, cookery and woodwork.

Life at Osborne House

The royal family established a regular pattern of visits to Osborne, usually visiting four times a year. The Queen loved fresh air, and spent as much time as possible outdoors, starting with breakfast. Her journal makes many references to the time she spent reading and writing under the shelter of trees or a small tent, in the grounds of the house. She also recorded her first experience of sea bathing:

'Drove down to the beach with my maid and went into a bathing machine, where I undressed and bathed in the sea (for the first time in my life) where a very nice woman attended me. I thought it was delight-

ABOVE Osborne House and grounds.
LEFT: Prince Albert and Queen Victoria, painted on porcelain, after Winterhalter.

ful until I put my head under water, when I thought I would be stifled.'
Queen Victoria's Journal, quoted in *Dear Osborne*, by John Matson

Prince Albert spent much of his time on managing the estate at Osborne, putting into practice his theories on landscaping, drainage and recycling. Each of the children looked after their own piece of garden. In the evenings, the family entertained themselves by putting on concerts and amateur dramatics, or by playing charades.

INFLUENCE OF ALBERT

Although the Prince was never completely accepted by British society, his influence on Victoria, the upbringing of their children, the running of the royal household and the encouragement of the arts and sciences in Britain was immense. He had a great interest in architecture, and was involved in several schemes, including the construction of Balmoral Castle and rebuilding at Buckingham Palace.

Albert was President of the Royal Society of Arts, which, under his leadership, staged the Great Exhibition of Arts and Manufacturers in 1851. This was the world's first international exhibition, set up in Hyde Park, London, in the Crystal Palace, a building specially designed in iron and glass. It aimed to celebrate the achievements in arts, industry and technology of Britain and her empire. The exhibition was a tremendous success. Six million people visited it, and proceeds from the tickets left a surplus. Prince Albert persuaded the government to use this money to purchase and develop land to the south of Hyde Park, building a series of institutions to promote the study of arts and sciences. The museum complex at South Kensington, and the Albert Hall, are the result of this initiative, which was not completed till after Albert's death.

The Albert Memorial

The death of Albert from typhoid in 1861 changed Victoria's life completely. She went into deep mourning, and led a very secluded life for the next ten years.
To commemorate her husband and

The Albert Memorial was recently restored by English Heritage.

his work, and as a focus for the nation's grief, a memorial was planned.

The winning design, chosen by the Queen, was by George Gilbert Scott, and was in the Gothic revival style. The centrepiece was an outsize bronze statue of the Prince, seated, with the catalogue of the Great Exhibition in his hand. The memorial contained dozens of statues, representing Albert's many different interests and works, including statues to agriculture, commerce, manufacture and engineering.

THE VICTORIAN FAMILY

The 'family' was one of the cornerstones of Victorian society, and provides a worthwhile focus for your pupils' investigation. The process of photography was invented by Fox Talbot in 1838, and taking photographs of family groups quickly became fashionable. By the 1880s, this popularity had spread to the lower levels of society. The spread of relatively cheap photographic studios encouraged even the poor to record their families for posterity.

Victoria and Albert with all their children, on the terrace at Osborne House in 1857.

CASE STUDY · VICTORIAN CIVIC PRIDE

VICTORIAN CIVIC PRIDE

The economic accomplishments of Britain during the nineteenth century made it a world dominating industrial power. The Victorians showed off this new confidence and wealth by building large imposing buildings, usually in city centres.

In 1835 a law was passed allowing towns and cities to administer their own affairs by the election of a town council. Previously, towns were run by the aristocracy - the local lord of the manor. Now many town councils embarked upon a redevelopment of their cities.

The Victorians believed in improving people's health and minds. To this end much of the redevelopment by town councils involved not just the provision of clean water supplies and effective sewage treatment, but also the building of museums, schools and colleges.

As the British Empire grew so the need for commercial organisations such as banks and insurance companies grew. Many were located in these new city centres.

BIRMINGHAM CITY CENTRE

During the nineteenth century Birmingham became a centre of manufacturing. It was known as 'the workshop of the world'. The city grew and became very wealthy. Factories were built and the population rapidly increased.

The new Council House in Council House Square around 1880. The square was later renamed Victoria Square.

Two new streets developed - Colmore Row and Waterloo Street. This photograph was taken in 1896.

New Street Station was opened in 1854. The station was enlarged in the 1880s.

This placed pressure on housing areas which became overcrowded slums with open sewers and polluted water supplies.

In 1838 Birmingham was granted a municipal charter of incorporation entitling it to elect its own town council. With administrative control of the city, the council

began to make improvements. Led by J H Chamberlain (below), it took control of the city's public utilities such as the water supply. The installation of pipes and pumping stations provided clean water across the city. The profits made from these municipal works paid for the redevelopment of the city centre.

In the 1850s to 1880s, the slums were cleared and a new city centre was created with new streets, for example Corporation Street and New Street. It contained civic buildings, shopping arcades, theatres, schools and colleges, commercial centres and railway stations.

WHAT EVIDENCE IS THERE OF VICTORIAN LIFE IN BIRMINGHAM CITY CENTRE?

Historical enquiry

You can use a question like this to frame your historical enquiry into an aspect of Victorian Britain. It will provide your pupils with the opportunity to investigate a

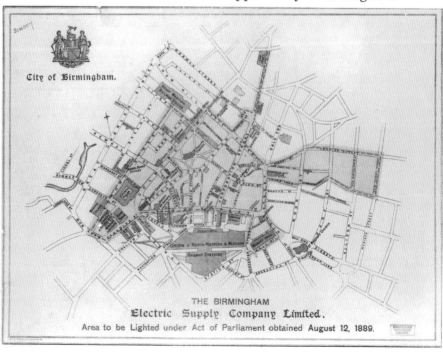

City of Birmingham.

THE BIRMINGHAM
Electric Supply Company Limited.
Area to be Lighted under Act of Parliament obtained August 12, 1889.

question using a variety of historical sources - to ask questions and to record their findings. You will find similar sources in your own locality.

Historical sources
Sources can be found in the Birmingham Central Library and by visiting the city centre.

Maps
Compare the 1889 map of Birmingham city centre with a modern map of the same area. What changes have occurred? What remains? What has disappeared? Look at the names of streets and buildings. What clues do they give of Victorian development? Why do you think these changes occurred? What does it tell us about the Victorians?

Photographs
Photographs of Birmingham's past and present can also be used to show change over time. They provide evidence of the life of the city centre and the people who lived and worked there.

Architecture
The Victorians favoured two types of architectural style for their civic buildings.

Classical: Similar style to Greek and Roman temples columns and porticos. Strong use of squares, circles and triangles.

Detail from the Council House.

Gothic: Narrow windows, turrets, bell towers and high gables. Pointed or perpendicular arches and 'mock' battlements.

Get pupils to look for these architectural styles as clues to dating a building. Occasionally buildings, as with the Council House, have a foundation stone. Encourage your pupils to look closely at a building because it can often provide many clues to answer their enquiry. Also ask pupils to look at the decoration on buildings as the Victorians often used decorative friezes on their civic buildings to show off their importance.

Monuments
In Birmingham city centre there are various monuments that you can use as evidence of Victorian

This statue of Queen Victoria (left) was originally carved in marble in 1901. It was cast in bronze and re-sited on this stone pedestal in 1951.

The Chamberlain memorial (right) was erected in 1880 and was designed by J H Chamberlain who was President of the Board of Trade.

development. The most obvious is the statue of Queen Victoria in Victoria Square. Another is the Chamberlain Memorial fountain in Chamberlain Square.

One of the entrances of Queen's College which commemorates a visit by Queen Victoria in 1887.

Names
The names of streets and buildings can be a clue to their history. Encourage pupils to gather evidence of names from maps and from observing names while visiting the city centre.

Corporation Street around 1899. Work began in 1878 to build this street, once a former slum area.

Part of Colmore Row today with a surviving Victorian building.

CASE STUDY — LIFE IN A COUNTRY HOUSE

Brodsworth Hall was built in 1861-63 by Charles Sabine Thellusson after inheriting a substantial sum of money in a family will. It was built in the Italianate style, replacing an earlier hall on the site.

The south (sunnier side) provided comfortable accommodation for the family while the north side contained the servants' wing, reusing materials from the earlier hall.

The garden is typically Victorian, consisting of mown lawns, formal flower gardens, a rose garden, a walled garden, a summer house and a quarry garden with a fern dell.

When the Hall was built fifteen servants were employed. However over time this number was reduced.

The entrance hall.

Different areas of the house segregated the family, their children and their servants. Even the male and female servants slept on different floors and had their own hierarchy depending upon status.

The entrance hall and the halls leading off it show the tastes and interests of the family. They are designed to impress and are used to display many possessions.

THE FAMILY AT LEISURE

Many rooms had a specific leisure function. In addition to a library and study, Brodsworth Hall has a Billiard Room and a Drawing Room. After dinner, ladies and gentlemen retired separately. The ladies would go to the Drawing Room, where music could be played and the men would go to the Billiard Room. This room would also be used to smoke and discuss mutual interests which, for the Thellusson family, would include racing and sailing. The Lathe Room was used by Charles Thellusson for his woodwork hobby.

The Billiard Room.

The garden was also used for recreation - walking, cycling, riding, sledging and skating. The Target House allowed the family to practise archery in bad weather, while in summer they would play croquet on the specially created lawn. The garden could also be a venue for social events such as family gatherings or garden parties.

Children too had their own particular living areas. These were well away from the main family rooms downstairs so that they would not disturb the adults or distract the servants.

THE SERVANTS AT WORK

When looking at the work of the servants it is useful to keep asking:

■ what has changed

■ what caused these changes

■ what effect did this have on the running of the Hall.

The Kitchen

The kitchen contains many mass-produced objects and basic labour-saving devices. They show how attempts were made to reduce the amount of manual labour an time needed for specific functions. These developments would ultimately require fewer servants and demonstrate the impact of mass production on working life.

Look particularly at:

■ cooking methods - what fuels and processes were used

Rather than trying to study everything in the kitchen give each pupil a specific item or problem to research. For example this late nineteenth-century refrigerator solves the problem of keeping food fresh and demonstrates advances in manufacturing processes. Explain what effect this item would have on the work of kitchen servants.

■ storage methods - how and where food was stored

■ which objects are still in use today and how have they changed

■ which gadgets are still in use and how have they been improved

■ what materials were used for cooking implements.

Contrast the room where food was prepared to the room where it was served and consumed by the family. Compare the utensils in the kitchen to those used in the dining room. How do they differ? Why do they differ? Would the servants use the crockery and cutlery in the dining room in the same way as those in the kitchen?

This room was used not only to entertain but also to impress. How can pupils tell this?

When the Hall was built there was no supply of water or source of power. Look at:

■ how the servants delivered cold and hot water to different rooms and then disposed of it. Originally there was only one bathroom. What does this suggest about sanitary arrangements? How pleasant would this be for the servants?

■ how would the servants have kept the Hall warm and well-lit. What specific tasks would be required? How easy would this have been? What were the implications for the servants of coal fires or oil lamps? What changes have occurred since the Hall was built?

This photograph highlights the different functions of a bedroom. Identifying each function will help show what tasks servants were expected to do. How does the level of comfort compare with a bedroom in the servants' wing?

Identify what technological achievements made life easier for the servants at Brodsworth, but at what eventual cost.

Woodlands Colliery Village

This village was built 1907-9 on Thellusson land to provide the workers of Brodsworth Main Colliery with improved living conditions. It was designed as a 'garden village' in the Arts and Crafts tradition and all houses have gardens. The houses are built of brick and in blocks of two to five. Some homes had a large living room, scullery and three bedrooms, others had a parlour, kitchen, scullery, three bedrooms and a bathroom. Land in the centre of the village was designated for a school, a co-operative store, an Anglican and a Wesleyan church and a Methodist chapel.

Aerial view of Woodlands. Note the symmetrical layout, indicative of a desire for order, and the enclosed green spaces, used for communal and recreational purposes.

BRITAIN SINCE 1930

The advantage of studying a period of history within living memory is that we can take advantage of primary sources from those who were actually there. There are photographs, newspapers, documentary films and the reminiscences of people who remember. There will also be many artefacts surviving from the period itself.

■ Look out for old photographs, newspapers and magazines

■ Speak to people you know

■ Search for interesting things connected with the war.

Valuable sources of information are local newspapers, often stored in the local library on microfilm. Pupils can use a number of different sources to study the social attitudes, wartime dangers and deprivation, financial problems, rationing and life after the war in the welfare state. Many people who remember the thirties and forties are only too willing to share their experiences and pupils can talk to them, ask questions and establish useful links. Your study could be based around the Second World War or could follow themes through a longer period. You will need to consider how lives in Britain changed as a result of the Second World War.

The house on the left, photographed in 1947, had been altered by 1960 (above). The front porch has been turned into a 'waiting room' for the Dental Surgery located in the front room. The balcony above has also been converted into a small bedroom. A canopy has been built above the new front door.

In 1947 a Kodak folding camera using 120 black and white roll film was used for family 'snaps'. By 1960 this had been replaced by a compact 35mm camera using colour slide film.

Look out for information in:

Libraries
Museums
Local Records Offices
Local History Libraries
Tourist Information Offices

Activity

What design features were included in a typical suburban 1930s' house?

Consider both inside and outside the house.

How were the new suburbs of the thirties different from the terraces of the Victorian period?

How would families have heated rooms and water?

Visit a typical thirties suburb in your town. Note the original features and the new additions.

Typical suburban house, South Croxton Road, London.

HOW HAVE PEOPLE'S LIVES CHANGED SINCE THE 1930s?

At home

In the 1930s it was possible to buy an average suburban semi-detached house for about £400. Mains water, gas and electricity were available in most towns although not in rural areas. Furniture was being produced on a large scale making it cheaper and more affordable. This enabled large numbers of people to furnish their homes in the new style which used pastel colours, geometric shapes and decorative motifs.

Many of the new houses of the 1930s had gardens and a garage even though most families did not possess a car. Although there was access to a better standard of living for many, unemployment and poverty were not far away. The economic depression and high unemployment were a constant threat to the new standard of living. Large areas of big cities suffered from high unemployment, poor housing and poverty.

The role of women

The main type of work for women in the 1930s was in domestic service, as shop assistants or in

A soldier, a farm worker and a land-girl at East Grinstead, May 1943.

offices. For many women, marriage meant automatic dismissal from their paid jobs, so most wives and mothers did not work outside the home. The outbreak of the Second World War brought a dramatic change to the lives of many women. As men were ordered to serve in the armed forces, their peacetime jobs still had to be done. Women had to do these jobs, many going out to work for the first time. The Women's Land Army was formed to fill the places of the thousands of farmworkers who had gone to serve in the armed forces. Millions of women went to work in factories and shipyards learning to do mechanics and engineering.

As the war continued women were called on to join the armed forces themselves and eventually most women between the ages of 18 and 50 were working towards the war effort. Only mothers with young children were exempt.

Leisure

In 1938, an Act of Parliament entitled a large number of workers to holiday pay which meant that for the first time, workers could go on holiday for a week without a loss of earnings. Many people were able to go on holiday for the first time. Holiday camps became popular and cheap rail travel gave people the opportunity of travelling further afield. Holidays abroad,

Roehampton Swimming Pool.

Broadcasting House, London.

however, were still rare and only began to gain in popularity from the 1950s onwards. At home, popular pastimes were gardening, following the cricket, football and tennis matches. Day trips and holiday excursions were also popular especially on Bank Holidays.

Radio and television

Listening to the radio became more frequent during the war. Radio broadcasts by the BBC were an invaluable source of information and entertainment and a large number of households had access to a wireless. The radio brought news of national and international events, sport and entertainment into the home. All types of information were available from medical advice to cooking ideas. Entertainment included comedy programmes. After the war, two new programmes were added - the Light Programme in 1945 and the Third Programme in 1946.

The BBC began a regular television service in 1936 which was suspended during the war but resumed in 1946. Initially there were very few viewers but television gradually gained in popularity and by the Coronation over 20 million people watched as Queen Elizabeth II was crowned. This was the first time such an event had

been televised and watched by so many. The increase of television in the 1950s led to the closure of hundreds of cinemas but it opened up a new cultural experience, which has had an increasing effect on our lives ever since.

Cinema

Cinema-goers grew from 20 million in the 1930s to 32 million after the war. Most films were in black and white but Technicolour was being introduced. In addition to the main film, cinema programmes included newsreels, general information films and often an organ

Odeon, Ramsgate.

recital by the resident organist! Cinema audiences soon dropped off when TV became common in the 1950s.

Health

In the 1930s, many places still had large areas with poor housing which caused illness and infectious diseases to spread quickly. Lack of money also led to a poor diet which caused yet more illness. Only the very poor were entitled to free medical treatment. Everyone else had to pay for medicines, staying in hospital, dental care and spectacles. Diphtheria and tuberculosis were still common and medical and dental care was still fairly basic in comparison with today's standards.

In 1948, the National Health Service was set up to care for all citizens in need of medical treatment. If the cost had stopped people from visiting a doctor or

dentist or optician before, it was no longer to be the reason. Drugs and treatment could be prescribed, regardless of the ability to pay. It was paid for out of taxes.

Transport

Despite petrol rationing and wartime priorities, motor car ownership grew from 1.7 million in 1938 to 4.4 million in 1950. The Road Traffic Act of 1934 introduced driving tests and in 1935 a 30 mph speed limit. The volume of traffic in the 1930s was very different to today. The new town plans created after the war included larger numbers of houses with their own garage.

Rationing

With the war, everyone could find a job which meant people now had money but they had nothing to spend it on! Supplies were rationed to ensure that everyone had a fair chance of obtaining basic foodstuffs and other items. Britain depended on imported foods and supply ships were vulnerable to attack, so food was in limited supply. Waste food, potato peelings and tea leaves were collected for pig swill. Old newspapers were used as wrapping paper. Clothes rationing was introduced because factories were turned over to making uniforms.

VOCABULARY

You will want to introduce your pupils to words which were common in the recent past but perhaps are no longer used, or their meaning has changed. For example:

allied	Anderson Shelter
blitz	censor
conscription	coupon
empire	evacuation
fascist	identity card
radar	rationing
recruit	refugee
GI	

EVENTS IN EUROPE

1929	Wall Street Crash leads to Great Depression of the 1930s
1933	Hitler gains power in Germany and starts to build up army, navy and airforce
1936	Jarrow Hunger March
	Abdication of Edward VIII
1937	Outbreak of Spanish Civil War
1938	Holidays with Pay Act
1939	Germany invades Poland
	National register set up. Identity cards issued
1940	Evacuation of children from British cities, food rationing
1940	Germany invades Denmark, Norway, Holland, Belgium and France
1940	British forces evacuated from France Dunkirk
	Italy declares war on Britain and France
	Start of war in North Africa
	Battle of Britain
	Blitz in Britain
	Food rationing begins
	Germany and Italy invade Yugoslavia and Greece
	1941 Germany invades Russia
	Japanese attack American fleet at Pearl Harbour
1942	Germans defeated in North Africa - El Alamein
	Millions of Jews murdered in concentration camps
	Baedeker raids on Britain's architectural heritage
1943	Main German army defeated in Russia
1944	Allies land in Normandy - D Day
	Most of France in Allied hands
	Russians advance on all fronts
	Heavy bombing of German cities
1945	Butler's Education Act Germans surrender. Hitler is dead
	Atom bombs dropped on Hiroshima and Nagasaki
	United Nations to be set up to keep world peace after the war
1946	Bread rationing
	Nuremberg Trials for war crimes
1947	Fuel crisis
1948	National Health Service
1949	NATO founded
1950	Outbreak of war in Korea
1951	The Festival of Britain
1954	No more food rationing!

FROM TOP: The Jarrow March, Plymouth in the blitz, Evening Standard 12 April, 1940, Newsboy, VE celebrations in London, 8 May 1945, The Festival of Britain, 1951.

CASE STUDY INVESTIGATING A LOCALITY

This case study looks at buildings, maps and other sources for the village of Buckminster in Leicestershire. It is taken from a survey of three Leicestershire villages by a local research group (see page 72). You may find similar published research in your area. If not you will be able to look out for buildings to investigate and a range of easily accessible associated sources in your local library or record office.

notice for 11 June 1873 says, "At the Buckminster Brick Yard the property of Mr Henson, Hovel boards, Planks, Brick Press, Well Sinking Frame, eight centres nine feet long, three Morticed Posts and Rails, 1000 Bundles of Reeds, Pantiles, Ridge Tiles and Bricks, quantity of Firewood and numerous effects."

Today: Brickyard pond is used for fishing and is a haven for wildlife.

BUCKMINSTER VILLAGE INSTITUTE

The Institute "for the benefit of the working men of Buckminster and the surrounding villages" was founded in 1886 and paid for by the Earl of Dysart, the local squire who owned the entire village. The Institute had a large playroom with billiards, bagatelle, draughts and dominoes; a reading room with London and provincial papers, a library of 250 books and a table and writing materials; a committee

room and caretaker's quarters. The annual subscription was 5s "but the committee have the power to admit lads and labourers at 1d per week".

Today: hall used is by local groups for meetings, as a polling station and for social gatherings.

BUCKMINSTER SCHOOL

This school building was completed in 1899 on a new site opposite the former school which had been constructed in 1841. The Earl of Dysart paid for its construction and it was named 'The Buckminster Unsectarian School'.

THE CRESCENT

The houses in The Crescent were built in 1892 replacing those in Bull Row which were put up in the 1830s. The census return for 1851 lists 166 people living here.

Today: houses are used mainly by estate workers and hardly altered.

BRICKYARD CLOSE

The tithe award map of 1841 shows this area pockmarked with ponds created by the digging of clay. The census return of 1841 lists Charles Hopkins and Thomas Parkinson as brickmakers. The sale

Cow Row.

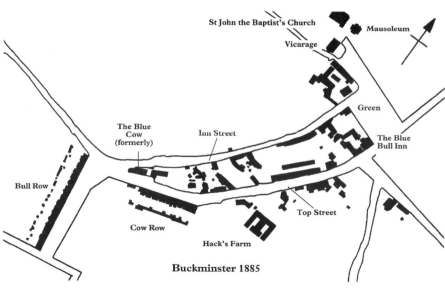

Buckminster 1885

A house for the Head teacher was built opposite the school.

Today: still the village school with building additions in 1989, and a temporary classroom added in 1997.

IVY HOUSE

This was once a public house called 'The Blue Bull'. Kelly's Post Office Directory of 1855 lists the landlord as Henry North and records that he was also a veterinary surgeon. The Blue Bull's licence was allowed to lapse at the wish of the Earl of Dysart. Its auction inventory contains a detailed inventory of each room and store.

Today: a private house.

Buckminster.
GENTRY.
Dysart Right Hon. Earl, Buckminster Hall
Lawson Rev. James, M.A. [vicar]
TRADERS.
Adcock John, 'Blue Cow,' baker & farmer
Ash George, butcher & shopkeeper
Bartram Richard, chairmaker
Bartram William, chairmaker
Beardsell Edward, grocer, seedsman, & agent to the East of England life assurance
Benson William, brick & tile maker
Brown John, tailor, & linen & woollen draper
Brown Richard, tailor
Burton John, bailiff to Earl Dysart
Coulson Thomas, cabinet maker
Exton John, farmer & grazier
Glassup Joseph, farmer & grazier
Hack William & Robert, farmers
Hand Thomas, farmer
Hill John, bricklayer

Hill Joseph, bricklayer
Manners Alfd. agent to Earl Dysart
Marshall Arthur, farmer & grazier
Marshall John, grazier
North Henry, 'Blue Bull,' & veterinary surgeon
Sharpe Southern, butcher
Spencer John, farmer & grazier
Stevens Thomas, boot & shoe maker, & shopkeeper
Watchorn Timothy, blacksmith
Weston Thos. saddler & harness maker
Woollerton William, boot & shoe maker
Sewstern.
Atter William, esq
Holmes Rev. Henry Courtley, M.A
TRADERS.
Almond John, cattle dealer
Bartram John, chairmaker
Bartram Joseph, carrier
Bowder William, farmer & grazier
Bright Benjamin Priestman, grocer
Burrows Wm. 'Waggon & Horses,' & frmr
Challand John, 'Red Lion'
Christain Esther (Mrs.), grazier

Christain Robert, farmer & grazier
Cramp William, carpenter
Doubleday Henry, farmer
Doubleday John, farmer
Dunmore William, carrier
Exton Thomas, farmer & grazier
Grice John, cattle dealer
Grice Mary (Mrs.), farmer
Grice Richard, 'Blue Dog'
Hardy John, grocer
Harvey Thomas, tailor & draper
Harvey William, shoemaker
Herring Thomas, farmer & grazier
North Joseph, blacksmith
Parker Mary (Mrs.), shopkeeper
Remington John, farmer
Robinson Samuel, boot & shoe maker
Royce Joseph, farmer & grazier
Royce Mark, horse dealer & farmer
Smith Thorpe, miller & baker
Thraves Samuel, tailor
Tinkler William, grazier
Townsend George, carpenter
Ward John, farmer
Wormell Mary (Mrs.), shopkeeper

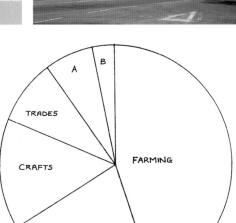

THE GREEN

An annual village feast was held on the Sunday after 6 July. The annual 'club day' of the local Buckminster Friendly Society turned into another feast day for the whole village from the 1880s. There was a church service and processions led by village bands from the area around. In 1859 the local Grantham Journal reported:

"In the evening the members paraded the village, the Band playing at most of the principal houses where they were regaled with plenty of 'Sir John Barleycorn'. All passed off quietly excepting one instance. A poor imbecile musician of the violin tribe who annoyed people by performing the part of 'Punch and Judy' got so drunk that he was obliged to be waited on by a gentleman in blue."

Levi Briggs ('imbecile musician') from the village of Skillington was charged with drunkenness and fined 5s.

Today: still an open space and the place for the annual Buckminster Festival.

BUCKMINSTER 1851 CENSUS

ANALYSIS OF EMPLOYMENT

FARMING – 45%

Farmers 6
Farmers Sons etc. (Working).... 3
Graziers 2
Agricultural Labourers........57
Farm Servants 6
Gamekeeper 1
Shepherd 1
Poultryman 1
Dairymaid 1
Waggoner 1
                            79

DOMESTIC – 21%

Servants 24
Gardeners 3
Housekeepers 3
Housemaids 2
Groom 1
Stableman 1
Watchman 1
Cook 1
Porter 1
Nursemaid 1
                            38

CRAFTS – 15%

Tailors (incl.1 J)............. 4
Dressmakers 4
Joiners 3
Carpenters 2
Chairmakers 2
Lace Runners 2
Lace Trimmer 1
Stonemason 1
Mason 1
Saddler 1
Harness Maker 1
Cooper 1
Brickmaker..................... 1
Cordwainer 1
Blacksmith 1
Shoemaker 1
                            27

A = PROFESSIONAL
B = UNEMPLOYED

TRADES – 9%

Grocers (incl.1A).. 4
Drapers 3
Bakers 2
Butchers 2
Innkeepers 2
Errand Boys 2
                 15

PROFESSIONAL – 7%

Land Agents 2
Writing Clerks..... 2
Schoolmistresses... 2
Schoolmaster 1
Vicar 1
Arbitor/Treasurer.. 1
Treasurer 1
Inspectress 1
Vice Inspector 1
Parish Clerk 1
                 13

UNEMPLOYED – 3%

Paupers....... 3
Independent... 1
Annuitant..... 1
             5

Note:A = Apprentice
J = Journeyman

CASE STUDY

THE IMPACT OF WAR

NATIONAL EVENTS - LOCAL STORIES

Everyone has seen films about the Second World War, with politicians and generals taking life and death decisions, the evacuation of Dunkirk, and battles being fought at sea, in the air and on land. But how can we relate these events and activities to the local area where we teach? Traces of the Second World War are all around us - in buildings and open spaces, in people's memories, in photographs and in official records. In fact there is so much information that sometimes the problem is one of selection from the vast mass available. Teachers, as well as pupils, can get bogged down in detail. The trick is to focus on a specific event or place that can provide a starting point for a thorough local investigation.

The last shell to fall on Dover

The town of Dover was in a vulnerable position after the fall of France in May 1940. The town was in firing range of shells from heavy German guns across the Channel as well as in danger from bombing raids. Shells could fall at any time of the day or night. The town was hit by 2,226 shells (compared with 464 bombs), making shells the more feared hazard.

The place where each shell or bomb fell was carefully noted. Towards the end of the war a map was published by the local newspaper, showing these locations. This information would have been classified during the war, but presumably, by 4 May 1945, just before VE day, these restrictions were lifted.

The map can tell us something about the vulnerability of Dover, and which streets are likely to have been substantially rebuilt after the war. But it tells us nothing about

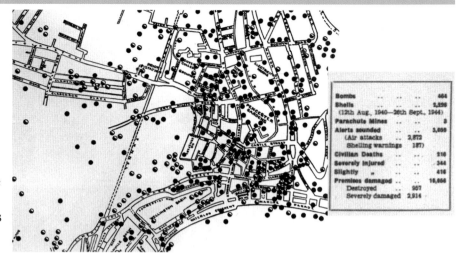

Extract from a map, originally published in the Dover Express, in May 1945 at the very end of the war, showing where bombs and shells fell in Dover.

what it was like to live in the town at that time, and gives no details about the physical effects of the shells and bombs.

When the last shell fell on Dover, no-one was aware that this really was the last one until afterwards. There are eye-witness accounts, although these are not very detailed, presumably because the event was not recalled until some time later.

All air raid damage was fully recorded as it happened. Dover, like other towns, was divided into sections, each with its own report centre. The Air Raid Precaution (ARP) personnel on duty would record, on specially printed forms,

I WAS THERE

Mr A.E. Whittamore remembers: *'I know where the last shell fell, because I was at the top of the street where it fell....I was at the top of Castle Street at the time, going home to where I lived down there....there was, I think it was an umbrella shop, Hubbards, there, and that's where the very last shell hit, on the very last day of shelling, which is the TSB bank now...I heard it fall and ran, although it was silly running after it fell....'*

the position of the occurrence, any damage to essential utilities, whether there was a fire, which services were on the spot, as well as the exact time of the event. Thus, when it was suggested that the shell which hit Hubbards umbrella shop was the 'last shell to hit Dover' it was possible to check in the records whether this was so.

Castle Street, Dover, today.

Castle Street today

Although a great deal of Dover has been completely rebuilt after the war, Castle Street is still quite recognisable, partly because of the landmark of Dover Castle. When you are asking your pupils to com-

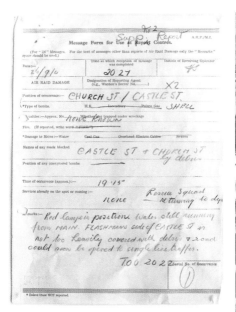

The ARP report, detailing damage done by the shell that fell on Castle Street.

pare old and new photographs, or old photographs with places, get them to look for easily identifiable buildings to orientate themselves. Get them to look up, above the ground floor. Roof lines and shapes are often a useful orientation device. Sometimes the remains of old painted advertising or shop names can be found on the sides of buildings. Sometimes you can see the line of an earlier

roof where an older building has been demolished. Comparing pre-war maps with modern equivalents can also help your pupils identify where the road layout has changed or where, for instance, a car park or open space replaced bomb-damaged buildings.

Shell damage in Castle Street. Later this was found to be the last shell to fall on Dover. The view of Dover Castle is very similar today.

DO YOU REMEMBER?

Memories of those who lived through the events of the Second World War help bring the more official records alive. Get your pupils to make a list of the questions they would like to ask someone about their experiences.

How old were you?
Where did you live?
Did you go to school? Was the school evacuated to a safe area?
What can you remember about the food? What did you miss?
Do you remember using an air raid shelter? What was it like?
Was your street damaged by bombs or shells?
What one memory or experience of the war would you like to tell us about?
Do you remember the end of the war?

Pupils can interview and record local residents or members of their own family to create their own oral history archive.

Bomb damage to Priory Gate Road, close to Dover Priory Station.
INSET: Priory Gate Road today, with the gap in the terrace of houses filled by a block of flats.

CASE STUDY   THE REMNANTS OF WAR

There is still plenty of evidence for the Second World War in Britain. How many examples can you spot in the place where you live?

BOMBING THE CITIES

Between the summer of 1940 and the spring of 1941 the Germans maintained aerial bombing raids on Britain. On the first night of the Blitz (from the German blitzkrieg meaning 'lightening war') nearly 2000 people were killed or injured in London. Apart from London, Birmingham, Manchester, Coventry, Liverpool, Plymouth,

Here's an air raid shelter converted into a fence!

Bristol and Glasgow were also key targets. In 1942 the Germans bombed Britain's historic cities, in particular Bath, Norwich, Canterbury, Exeter and York. The air raids were nicknamed the 'Baedeker raids' on the

This street in Southampton shows evidence of where one bomb fell. This terrace of houses, built around 1900, has had a single bombed house replaced in a different style.

assumption that the Luftwaffe had consulted the cultural guidebooks for locations.

This aerial photograph was taken by the RAF in 1948 and shows the damage caused by war-time bombing raids on Coventry. On the night of November 14, 1940 German bombs destroyed 40 acres (16 ha.) of the city. The front of the cathedral you can see here was left as an approach to a newly-built cathedral.

An air raid shelter converted into a shed.

SHELTERING FROM ENEMY BOMBS

Air raid shelters like this one were built in thousands of gardens across the country. Many were dismantled after the war but others have survived as reminders of the conflict.

This pillbox near Harwich guarded inland routes.

GUARDING THE LAND

When it was thought that the German army would cross over the Channel to Britain, a whole series of defences were put in to stop, or slow down, an invasion. 'Pill-boxes' of reinforced concrete were built for soldiers to guard strategic points, such as river crossings.

REMEMBERING THE WAR HONOURING THE DEAD

Almost every town and village has a war memorial commemorating the dead of the two World Wars. Memorials were often placed at important places in the locality, such as at crossroads, in churchyards or in public parks and squares.

This is part of a report in the local newspaper for Harwich, Essex in May 1919,

'A meeting was held in the vestry of Harwich Church to consider the question of a war memorial to the men and women connected with Harwich Parish Church who fell in the war, and also what form this memorial should take. Many suggestions were made including a clock, a brass plate inside the church, a stained glass window in the east of the church and there was also a suggestion to put a large cross in the churchyard like many churches were doing. The putting up of an artistic oak screen in front of the chancel appeared the most popular of the suggestions, and it was unanimously decided.'

Roads were often named after people or events of the war. This one commemorates a famous general who commanded the Eighth Army in North Africa.

The dedication ceremony for an Essex village memorial in 1920.

In 1946 the war memorial was re-dedicated to the dead of the Second World War.

THE CASE OF THE MISSING RAILINGS

Iron railings outside houses were removed to be melted down and transformed into tanks, guns and ammunition. This picture was taken in April 1940 in Chalk Farm, London.

Look out for the evidence of where the iron railings once were. Sometimes the lead which held the railings in place survives.

FURTHER READING AND INFORMATION

★ indicates resources suitable for pupils

🎦 indicates video

\# indicates the English Heritage Education on Site series for teachers. The series includes titles on local studies (such as *Using Historic Parks and Gardens*), historic sites (such as *Using Castles* and *Using Industrial Sites*), National Curriculum subjects (such as *Art and the Historic Environment*) and other aspects of teaching and learning (such as *History through role play*). The full range of English Heritage Education titles is included in our catalogue, *Resources* (information on page 72).

General

🎦 *The Big History Action Pack*, English Heritage, 75 minutes 1999. A journey of discovery into England's history, packed with activities to engage children's interest in the past, in or out of school.★

Corbishley, M, Gillingham, J, Kelly, R, Dawson, I & Mason, J, *The Young Oxford History of Britain & Ireland*, Oxford University Press, 1996. ISBN 0-19-910035-7. From the earliest prehistory to the 1990s.★

🎦 *Teaching Primary History*, English Heritage, 58 minutes, 1998. An in-service video which reflects on successful practice in teaching classroom history in recent years.

🎦 *The Key Stage 1 Curriculum*, English Heritage, 19 minutes, 1991. This in-service video follows a school planning a visit to a seventeenth-century house with follow-up in the classroom and evaluation.

Local environment

David, R, *History at Home*, English Heritage, 1996. ISBN 1-85074-591-9. Activity ideas for parents and teachers to use in studying their immediate locality with children.# 🎦 *History at Home: family detectives finding the past* is presented by David Bellamy. English Heritage, 18 minutes, 1995.

🎦 *Doorstep Discovery: working on a local history study*. English Heritage, 30 minutes, 1993. Follows a group of trainee teachers carrying out local history studies around their college and on teaching practice in a primary school.

🎦 *Investigating History*. Two programmes with teacher's notes and photocopiable sheets looking at work on ancient sites and in the locality. Produced by the BBC in association with English Heritage, 58 minutes, 1995.

Issues

Barnicoat, J, *Newspapers and Conservation*, English Heritage, 1994. ISBN 1-85074-511-0.# Keith, C, *Using Listed Buildings*, English Heritage, 1991. ISBN 1-85074-297-9. Introduces the complex and sometimes conflicting issues in the protection of the historic buildings.

Recording gravestones

Mytum, H, *Recording and analysing gravestones*, Council for British Archaeology, early 2000. ISBN 1-902771-09-5. Contains an example of the gravestone recording form.

Objects

Durbin, G, Morris, S & Wilkinson, S, *Learning from objects*, English Heritage, 1990. ISBN 1-85974-259-6.#

🎦 *Archaeological Detectives*, four A3-poster games and a video, English Heritage, 79 minutes, 1990/91.★

Documents

Davies, I & Webb, C, *Using Documents*, English Heritage, 1996. ISBN 1-85074-492-0.#

Purkis, S, *Using School Buildings*, English Heritage, 1993. ISBN 1-85074-379-7.#

Photographs

Copeland, T, *Teacher's handbook for Local Studies*, National Monuments Record, 1998. ISBN 1-873592-37-X. A guide to using aerial photographs and local buildings.

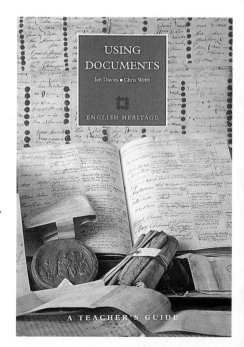

Interpreting history

📹 *According to the Evidence*, English Heritage, 30 minutes, 1998. Looks at the way in which

evidence for the past is presented. Some sequences for classroom showing.

Interpreting the Past, English Heritage, 1999. ISBN 1-85074-737-7. Pack of 6 A3 full colour posters for the classroom with an illustrated booklet of notes for teachers.

Looking at houses

Allen, S, Hollinshead, L & Wilkinson, S, *Using Houses and Homes*, English Heritage, 1998.

ISBN 1-85074-398-3.#

Barden, H, *Houses and Homes*, Wayland, 1994. ISBN 1-7502-0331- 5.★

Durbin, G, *Using Historic Houses*, English Heritage, 1993. ISBN 1-85074-390-8.#

Gee, A, *Looking at Houses*, Batsford, 1983. ISBN 0-7134-0845-6.★

Storytelling

Maddern, E, *Storytelling at Historic Sites*, English Heritage, 1992. ISBN 1-85074-378-9.# 2x90 minute cassettes also available.

Romans

Roman Britain Poster Pack, 8 A3 full-colour posters, English

Heritage, 1997. ISBN 1-85074-692-3.

Corbishley, M & Cooper, M, *Real Romans: digital*

time traveller, TAG & English Heritage, 1999. ISBN 1-9028-0400-7. Introducing the Romans through a cartoon-illustrated book and CD-ROM featuring Housesteads fort, Wroxeter city and Lullingstone villa.★

Corbishley, M, *What do we know about the Romans?*, Wayland, 1993. ISBN 0-7500-0852-0.★

Watson, I, *Using Roman Sites*, English Heritage, 1997. ISBN 1-85074-334-7.#

Watson, I, *A teacher's handbook to Hadrian's Wall*, English Heritage, 1997. ISBN 1-85074-375-4.

Watson, I, *A teacher's handbook to Lullingstone Roman Villa*, English Heritage, 1998. ISBN 1-85074-684-2. For information about visiting Lullingstone see page 72.

📹 *Talkin' Roman*, English Heritage, 25 minutes, 1996.★

Anglo-Saxons

📹 *Talkin' Saxon*, English Heritage, 20 minutes, 1997.★

Stoppleman, M, *Anglo-Saxon Village*, A & C Black, 1994. ISBN 0-7136-3813-3.★ The story of West Stow. For information about visiting West Stow and the resources/service for teachers contact: West Stow Country Park and Anglo-Saxon Village, The Visitor Centre, Icklingham Road, West Stow, Bury St Edmunds, Suffolk, IP28 6HG. Tel: 01284 728718.

Vikings

📹 *Talkin' Viking*, English Heritage, 25 minutes, 1998.★

Hall, R, *Viking York*, Batsford/English Heritage, 1996. ISBN 0-7134-7720-2.

Richards, J, *Viking Age England*, Batsford/English Heritage, 1991. ISBN 0-7134-6519-0.

Tolhurst, M, *Viking Street*, A & C Black, 1994. ISBN 0-7136-3814-1.★ For information about visiting the Jorvik Viking Centre and the Archaeological Resource Centre and the resources/service for teachers contact 01904 543 402.

Tudors

Bagenal, A & M, Tudor England, Longman, 1987. ISBN 0-582-18828-8.★

Girouard, M, *Life in the English Country House*, Penguin, 1980. ISBN 0-14-00-5406-5.

Reynoldson, F, *The Tudors: History starts here*, Wayland, 1999. ISBN 0-7502-2364-2.★

Yaxley, S, *Tudor Home Life: The way it was*, Chambers, 1980. ISBN 0-550-755300-6.★

For information about visiting Kirby Hall (English Heritage) see page 72.

Victorians

Allen, E, *Civic Pride*, A & C Black, 1979. ISBN 0-7136-1896-5.★

Girouard, M, *The Victorian Country House*, Yale University Press, 1979. ISBN 0-300-034572-5.

Life on a Royal Estate: A document pack for Osborne House, English Heritage, 1986. ISBN 1-85074-126-3. 39 facsimile documents with teacher's notes.

Little, B, *Birmingham Buildings: The Architectural Story of a Midlands City*, David & Charles, 1971. ISBN 0-7153-5295-4.

Overy, C, *A teacher's guide to Charles Darwin: his life, journeys and discoveries*, English Heritage,

1997. ISBN 1-85074-688-0.

📼 *Paws on the Past*, English Heritage, 20 minutes, 1996. KS1 pupils investigate life in a Victorian country house.★

Tolhurst, M, *A teacher's handbook to Osborne House*, English Heritage, 1990. ISBN 1-85074-289-8.

Victorians at Work, National Monuments Record, 1998. ISBN 1-873592-43-4. 8 A3 photographs with teacher's notes.

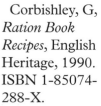

Victorian Transport, English Heritage, 1999. ISBN 1-873592-46-9. 8 A3 photographs with teacher's notes.

Wood, R, *Family Life in Victorian Britain*, Wayland, 1994. ISBN 0-7502-1008-7.★

For information about visiting Brodsworth Hall, Down House and Osborne House (English Heritage) see below.

Mid-century Britain

Allen, E, *Wartime Children 1939-1945*, A & C Black, 1983. ISBN 0-7136-1503-6.★

Britain since 1930, National Monuments Record, 1998. ISBN 1-873592-44-2. 8 A3 photographs with teacher's notes.

Corbishley, G, *Ration Book Recipes*, English Heritage, 1990. ISBN 1-85074-288-X.

Corbishley, G, *Appetite for Change: food and cooking in twentieth-century Britain*, English Heritage, 1993. ISBN 1-85074-400-9.

📼 *The Milk Jug Mystery*, English Heritage, 20 minutes, 1997. KS1

pupils comparing life today with the late 1940s.★

Parsons, M, *Rationing*, Wayland, 1999. ISBN 0-7502-2400-2.★

Local studies

Clinton, D, *When Bacon was Sixpence a Pound: Victorian Life in Buckminster, Sewstern and Sproxton*, Workers Educational Association, 1989.

Planel, P, *Battlefields, defence, conflict and warfare*, English Heritage, 1995. ISBN 1-85074-590-0.#

Purkis, S, *Using memorials*, English Heritage, 1995. ISBN 1-85074-493-9.#

Willis, H, *Pill-boxes*, Secker & Warburg, 1985. ISBN 0-43657-360-1.

Organisations

The Historical Association was founded in 1906 to bring together people who share an interest in the past. It promotes and assists the study of history at all levels and is very active in primary education. Membership gives the magazine 'Primary History' and many other benefits. For information contact: The Historical Association, 59a Kennington Park Road, London SE11 4JH. Tel: 0171 735 3901. Email: enquiry@history.org.uk WEB site www.history.org.uk

Young Archaeologists Club is open to all 9-16 year olds and gives a regular magazine, local branches, archaeological holidays and the National Archaeology Days. For information contact: Young Archaeologists Club, Council for British Archaeology, Bowes Morrell House, 111 Walmgate, York YO1 2UA. Tel: 01904

671417. Email: archaeology@compuserve.com

The Council for British Archaeology also provides a service and publications for teachers. WEB site www.britarch.ac.uk/cha